Some early praise for Jim Joseph's new book,
The Personal Experience Effect:

"Brand experience guru Jim Joseph adds a fifth element to the classic four P's of marketing: personality. Among the most successful brands are those indelibly tied to the personality behind it. If you're an entrepreneur, or building your personal brand for any reason, read this book and learn how to develop one of the most important essentials to everlasting brand success: the personal experience."
Melanie Notkin, Founder and Creator of Savvy Auntie

"Fasten your seat belts! Jim Joseph's *The Personal Experience Effect* s a road map to navigating your personal brand, at your own speed, focusing on all aspects of your life. It is a game changer!"
Sandi McKenna, Co-Host of MidLife Road Trip

"I had never thought of myself as a brand until I met Jim Joseph on Twitter. His advice on branding has helped me take Family Foodie from blog to business. Thinking of yourself as a brand will not only change the way you do business, it will change your future."
Isabel Laessig, Blogger at FamilyFoodie.com and Founder of the Sunday Supper Movement

"It's exciting to see Jim Joseph extend his Experience Effect strategies to personal branding. Individuals create experiences, yet the idea of personal branding can be elusive for people. By using examples of well-known individuals, Jim offers concrete ways readers can learn from and adapt what celebrities have done to strengthen the integral experiences they create with their own personal brands."
Mike Brown, The Brainzooming Group

The Personal Experience Effect

Big Brand Theory Applied to Personal Life

By Jim Joseph
Author of the award-winning
The Experience Effect and
*The Experience Effect
for Small Business*
http://JimJosephExp.com
@JimJosephExp

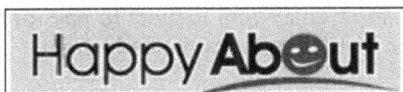

Happy About

20660 Stevens Creek Blvd., Suite 210
Cupertino, CA 95014

Published by Happy About®
20660 Stevens Creek Blvd., Suite 210, Cupertino, CA 95014
http://happyabout.com

First Printing: August 2013
Hardcover ISBN: 978-1-60005-241-5 (1-60005-241-X)
eBook ISBN: 978-1-60005-242-2 (1-60005-242-8)
Place of Publication: Silicon Valley, California, USA
Hardcover Library of Congress Number: 2013936818

Trademarks

Warning and Disclaimer

Dedication

With love and appreciation to the best part of my brand: Christopher, Alicia, JP, and Sophie

Acknowledgments

I'd like to thank all the people in my life who have made up my personal brand. If surrounding yourself with all the right people is a key ingredient for your life, then I have done something right.

My family and friends: my daily motivation to keep up this crazy pace. I can't thank you enough for everything you do for me.

ESM High School: my childhood friends taught me what love and support is at the beginning of it all. It's wonderful to stay connected in social media.

Cornell and The Pikes: four of the most happiest years of my life, and the institutions that shaped who I am today.

Johnson & Johnson: my first foray into brand management proved my love of marketing with mentorship I was so fortunate to receive and still use every day.

CPPartners: my entrepreneur streak with a team that couldn't be beat brought in amazing results.

Colleagues through the years: a constant stream of support and guidance that consistently makes a difference each and every time.

My team at Cohn & Wolfe: incredible intelligence, creativity, and commitment that never cease to amaze.

My editor at *Entrepreneur*: thank you for helping to continually hone my storytelling skills.

My friends at Happy About: I so appreciate the continual vote of confidence and help getting this all done.

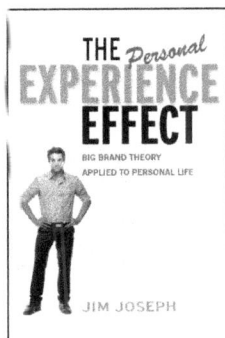

http://JimJosephExp.com

Contents

Foreword | Make an Entrance
Robert Verdi 1

Prologue | So I Got to Thinking
*Big Brand Theory Applied to Personal
Life* 11

Introduction | Become a Brand
Steve Jobs 17

Chapter 1 | Learn *The Experience Effect*
Donna Summer 33

Chapter 2 | Create Who You Want to Be
J. K. Rowling 41

Chapter 3 | Position Yourself
Meryl Streep 51

Chapter 4 | Make Good Choices
James Carville 71

Chapter 5 | Understand Your Audience
Jillian Michaels 79

Chapter 6 | Make a Plan
Julia Child 87

Chapter 7 | Ensure Consistency
Abraham Lincoln 97

Chapter 8 | Know What You Need
Kim Kardashian 107

Chapter 9 | Be Flexible
Hillary Rodham Clinton 117

Chapter 10	Own the Digital World *Michael J. Fox* 129
Chapter 11	Find Your Voice, Choose Your Look *Jack Welch* 137
Chapter 12	Go to Market *Cher* 147
Chapter 13	Surround Yourself *Arnold Schwarzenegger* 155
Chapter 14	Make Your Mark *TOMS Shoes* 165
Epilogue	A Story of Inspiration *Two Tweets, One Brand* 171
Author	About Jim Joseph *A Builder and a Fixer.*................. 179
Books	Other THiNKaha® Books 183

Make an Entrance

By Robert Verdi, Famed Lifestyle Expert

I remember the very first time I met Jim Joseph.

At the time, he was the president of a prestigious public relations agency whose roster of clients included some of the most important beauty and fashion brands in the country. I was already nervous when I arrived at his office, and then his assistant brought me into a large, intimidating conference room where I awaited his arrival. Jim entered the room with his shoulder-length salt and pepper hair and a very colorful Paul Smith shirt, topped off with an ear-to-ear smile. I was pleasantly surprised and was immediately put at ease.

Not only had Jim entered the room, but his brand did as well. I was expecting the president of a leading PR firm to be wearing a traditional dark suit. I also anticipated that when he arrived, his personality would match his dark suit and he would be very buttoned-up and all about business. What I got was the exact opposite.

The Jim Joseph brand is forward thinking and modern. He was down-to-earth and friendly—he told me that he was a big fan of mine and that he always wanted to meet me. Without hesitation, Jim told me that his fabulously fashionable shirt of choice that day was inspired by our upcoming meeting, and he asked me if I approved of the choice. All of this was very disarming.

I later learned that Jim has the same demeanor with everyone he meets, and he has a closet filled with fabulous shirts—they are his signature and a part of his brand. I believed that Jim had gone above and beyond just for me, yet he didn't even know me.

There you have it, some of the core qualities of the Jim Joseph brand: original, friendly, and personalized—just for you.

Those qualities are some of the ingredients that have helped shape Jim's brilliance and success as a leading marketer. If you meet with him, you will want to work with him. He knows that and he has built a tremendous reputation (and personal brand) around the ability he has to create that feeling. Since that day, I've worked on many projects with Jim and he has become one of my mentors, offering me great advice and counsel as I continue to build my "Robert Verdi" brand.

There is no better person than Jim Joseph to guide you on your personal mission to begin building a career, or even reinventing yourself by thinking about yourself as a brand. Jim's experience in helping develop and market brands big and small is unparalleled.

While the idea of packaging your ideas and becoming a brand may seem challenging, with Jim as your guide you will be amazed as you unfold your ideas reading this book. You will create your brand identity and it will become a manual to your life, helping you redefine how you approach everyday challenges. Whether looking for a job or looking for love, your personal brand and your understanding of what that brand means are tools for success in all aspects of your life.

In his first two books, *The Experience Effect* and *The Experience Effect for Small Business*, Jim illustrates why consumers care deeply about the overall experience of the buying process and how they respond to all the various marketing messages. He teaches us that when the brand's marketing elements come together to form a seamless experience, the customer is left with a feeling of satisfaction that ultimately builds loyalty. Jim Joseph calls this ideal combination "the experience effect."

What is the effect? It's when a simple yet powerful brand experience resonates purposefully, consistently, and continuously with customers. Jim took his big business brand theories, applied them to small businesses, and now he applies them to your life.

In *The Personal Experience Effect*, Jim breaks down brand development into several categories. He cites uniquely successful examples of personal branding across many industries. He illustrates how people use their platforms in pop culture as individual brand marketers practically bottling the essence of their ideas and the feelings that people get from each one of them.

This is the genius used by people who have developed themselves strategically as products. From J.K. Rowling to Kim Kardashian to Hillary Clinton, Jim explains their brands to us, and teaches us how to recognize our own unique brand DNA so that we can create the professional and personal outcome each of us wants in our lives.

Yes, it's true—you, too are a brand.

In this challenging economic environment, it has become not only evident but important for you to understand how to shape your own personal brand. *The Personal Experience Effect* will help you define, refine, and cultivate your very own brand DNA that will help you build your professional life with greater understanding, purpose, and meaning. As each and every industry has become more and more hypercompetitive, it has become increasingly more important to brand yourself. You must understand what it is that makes you unique, what makes you great, and what makes you stand out in a sea of millions. Thankfully, *The Personal Experience Effect* makes it easy for you to understand how to take the steps necessary to identify the qualities and characteristics that will allow you to discover the essence of your very own personal brand.

For me, my brand just sort of happened.

But in order to maintain it and further develop it, I've had to examine what makes my brand unique and special among others. I've discovered that my personal branding recipe has three important ingredients: good taste, everyday luxury, and humor.

I'm also a skilled connector—I have an enviable database chock full of celebrities, socialites, divas, dignitaries, designers, and more. However, as a fashion personality, the single most defining quality of my brand is my sense of humor. It is not only what makes me distinct, it is the tool that I use to seduce, disarm, entertain, and inform people about the world I embody: the world of fashion.

Being funny is the cornerstone of my success in television as well as my success as a celebrity stylist. It's why people want to listen to what I have to say and why celebrities love having me in their entourage. My sense of humor above all other qualities is what makes me stand out. Many other fashion insiders are celebrated merely for their affiliations with prestigious publications, not their own personalities.

Not me. I want us to have fun while I'm helping you navigate through the latest fashion trends and decide which of them you need to buy this season. I wholeheartedly believe that fashion should be fun and should not be intimidating. Let's face it: you have to get dressed to go to work everyday, so why should getting dressed be another job? It shouldn't! It should be easy and stress free, especially since it has to happen everyday, sometimes twice a day. Naked is generally not an option.

Jim says this is my "positioning," and you'll learn how to develop your own.

For some, another important aspect of building your personal brand will be identifying a signature trademark. I can't deny the impact that wearing my sunglasses has had on my brand development. The single biggest effect those sunglasses perched atop my shiny dome has offered is simply allowing me to be more recognizable among the other fashion experts.

Jim says this is my "own-able branding element," and you'll learn how to develop your own.

People who may not know me by name can recognize me by this description: "the tall, skinny bald guy with the sunglasses." I have used these kinds of guidelines in *The Personal Experience Effect* to galvanize my brand identity. Having Jim's guidance through this book makes the process less stressful and more successful for me, and now for everyone.

I keep Jim Joseph on speed dial. Project to project, concept to concept, and idea to idea, I check in with one of my favorite, dependable, astute mentors. His quick insights are often used to help me shape my next steps—steps that are now made easy for you with his book.

It is a unique time that we are living. One where you can invent yourself and write your own ticket to success by applying branding strategies that have forever been used by major marketers.

We are living in the most exciting time: the digital age. You can use your ideas and feelings to customize your life and create an overall experience for everyone you interact with. You can create content that connects you to the world. Yes, your voice can echo through the hallways of Facebook, Twitter, Instagram, LinkedIn, and blogs where you can make your presence consistent and dependable. You have the power to create a seamless experience in the world with your very own personal brand.

Remember this very important lesson: don't just walk into a room, make an entrance and smile—it works for Jim Joseph every time.

Robert Verdi

Robert Verdi is one of the nation's leading lifestyle experts. He has hosted five television series including his own self-titled reality show. He is one of the most respected fashion pundits commenting on pop culture and he is inextricably linked to many of today's most famous and loved celebrities.

So I Got to Thinking

Big Brand Theory Applied to Personal Life

I am a marketing guy, a big brand marketing guy. Spent my entire career honing my craft by making sure I got experience working on a variety of brands in a mix of categories across a range of consumer targets. I don't want to say that I've seen it all, but there are days when it certainly feels like it.

I'm one of those people who knew at a young age that I wanted to go into marketing. Not sure I even knew what it was, but I knew that it was for me. I would watch the television commercials more than the actual television shows, and I would look at the print ads more than read the actual magazine articles.

I just loved looking at all the brands and what they had to say. Maybe it was "and she told two friends" commercial that really did it, I'm not sure (clearly a bit of foreshadowing for today's social media).

When I finally got into marketing after grad school, I pretty quickly became a new products expert by launching a bunch of new products at Johnson & Johnson. I later got bit by the entrepreneurial bug and started my own agency. I'm not sure how I had the guts to do it, but I saw an opportunity in the market, and I seized it.

That little agency was among the first to start building brand websites back in the day; we were super creative, and we were on top of the world. I then sold the agency to the Publicis Groupe and got the chance to help even more clients solve their marketing challenges within a much larger multinational organization.

After what feels like a million brand assignments and many an agency merger, I finally wrote my first book in 2010. *The Experience Effect* is really a compilation of all my marketing experiences to date, and it helped me commit to paper what big brand marketing is all about and how to do it well. I think of it as my big brand theory brought to life.

Through all of these experiences, I developed my personal brand as a marketer, reflected in every single career move and every marketing assignment and, of course, in my personal life as well as a partner and also a father of two.

The *funny* thing is that I was writing the book just as the economy started to unravel around all of us. People were losing jobs left and right, and many people found themselves stuck. Stuck in a place either they didn't want to be, or stuck in a place that they didn't realize would become long-term.

Raises disappeared, bonuses evaporated, and promotions were long put on hold. Careers stalled all around us, and we were all standing in place, or at least that's what it felt like.

So while I was writing a book about big brand marketing, I was watching people struggle with their lives and their careers. As I watched people wrestle with career and personal decisions, many of which were totally unplanned, I began to realize one thing.

We are all brands too.

Personal branding isn't necessarily a new concept, but it was suddenly cast in a new light for me. It suddenly had a new purpose, and a new urgency.

So it got me thinking that maybe we can market ourselves to a new place—the place we've always wanted to be! It's just marketing after all, and not that different from a lot of the big brand marketing I'd been doing for years.

Much of this is no different than marketing a brand like Tide or Levi's.

The choices we all make in life are no different than the choices that brands make when marketing their products. The stakes are more personal and perhaps higher, but the process is nearly the same.

At least that was my theory.

So I planned to write a third book—another follow-up to my original *The Experience Effect*—that takes the principles of big brand marketing and applies them to real people.

My second book focused on small business, so I decided it was time to tackle people—individuals need the help just as much. I decided to write a book that can help people market themselves so that they can make tough decisions to get what they want. Not just on the career front, but on the personal side too.

Hence, *The Personal Experience Effect.*

I hope you find this book helpful in gaining an understanding of who you are and what you want out of life, both personally and professionally.

I hope you start thinking of yourself as a brand.

We will start by defining our personal brand, just like the big brands do, and then we'll determine how best to market it. The result will be the attainment of your personal goals.

The happy ending, as they say, is your very own *Personal Experience Effect.*

I hope you enjoy it.

Become a Brand

Just like any other morning, I woke up today and almost instantly started interacting with brands. Gillette personal products, an early morning Diet Pepsi, Nike workout gear, iPad to check e-mail, a colorful Paul Smith shirt, and a Starbucks on the way to work—just to name a few.

We live with brands all day long, every day of our lives. We've incorporated them into our lives because in one way or another, we have determined that they help us. They make life easier, more rewarding, and more tasteful—whatever the case may be. This is true of all the brands across every spectrum of our lives—from food to fashion, from home to personal care.

Most of us don't even realize that this is happening. We've let a collection of brands into our lives very subconsciously yet, at the same time, for a definitive purpose that we may not even think about.

Diet Pepsi gets me going in the morning. It's a bold snap of refreshment in a really cold can that gives me a jolt. It helps me get to the gym every morning at 5:15 a.m.

Nike helps me feel as if I'm young and fit, even though clearly that is an ongoing battle. Wearing Nike gives me the edge I need to go running in the rain or to work out an extra fifteen minutes, so early each day!

Apple keeps me connected and makes me feel as if I'm on the cutting edge. It helps me get my work done, stay connected to friends, and ride on the pulse of pop culture. I wrote this book on an Apple laptop.

Paul Smith gives me some personal style, something I want to set me apart.

Starbucks is a friendly start to what can often be a long day. The baristas know me there, and they start making my drink the moment I walk through the door. I simple have to say whether I want hot or cold.

Each of these brands adds value to my life, so I keep them close at hand. I have them positioned in my mind for what they do for me.

- Diet Pepsi: wake-up call to get going in the morning

- Nike: gear to stay young

- Apple: tools to stay connected

I'm not sure this is how the brands want me to position them, but it is how they have come to add value to my life.

Positioning? We'll get to that later.

As a result, I have grown to love these brands, and I am extremely loyal to them. I will go out of my way to find a Diet Peps over a Diet Coke.

The only way to explain that is that there is some sort of an emotional connection that transcends the simple need to drink something. It's the emotional connection that creates a brand, and it means so much more than just any product.

So how is this at all relevant to you?

Well, this is exactly what it means to be a brand.

Brands transcend the products themselves and become much more meaningful to their consumers than just the physical benefits. Diet Pepsi means so much more to me than just a beverage.

Nike means so much more than just a pair of running shorts.

To those who love you, you are so much more than just another ordinary person.

The same is true of people, and the same is true of you. In addition to my Diet Pepsi, I engaged with some people this morning too, including my teenage son, and he is quite the guy!

We incorporate people into our lives, often without realizing it, for many of the same reasons that we incorporate brands.

We meet them, we get to know them, we position them in our minds, and we ultimately let them into our lives because they add value to us. Hopefully we end up loving them for it. Family and friends, work colleagues and associates, neighbors and acquaintances. We may not realize it, but we evaluate all of them based on their brands.

We bring people into our lives because they make things easier, more rewarding, and more tasteful, whatever the case may be. Just like brands, we add people into our lives because of the value they bring to us.

Think of your friends. If you stop and think about it, they each give you something in your life. In this way, people are no different than brands. In fact, people are brands, which is the whole point.

Each person in our life is there because we have a perception of what they will offer us. Over time we have learned who they are and what they are all about. We have seen their behaviors and the decisions that they have made, and we have either grown to appreciate them for it, or we have realized that they no longer belong alongside us. Our perceptions of people have been shaped by the decisions that they have made in their lives, and how they affect us.

Even our children.

They are a part of our lives because we have brought them in. They too add value, even though there are days when that doesn't feel like the case. They too are brands, just in development. At least that's what I told my son as we were filling out college applications!

In this regard, hopefully you see that marketing is all about choices.

When our choices and decisions consistently make up a pattern of behavior, then we start to position a person in our mind as some sort of a reflection of that behavior. We give him an identity, and then we watch to see if everything he does stacks up to how we perceive him/her.

As a result, we have turned these people into brands. It's human nature, and we can't help ourselves. I just don't know if we've ever talked about it this way or have ever pegged it as branding.

The more consistent the behavior and the more consistent the decisions made throughout life, then the more clear-cut the person's brand and the more definitively we know how to incorporate him/her into our lives.

That, my friends, is the essence of the experience effect. *The Personal Experience Effect* to be exact, as it relates to personal branding.

Allow me to illustrate with a few examples.

The Career Coach

In every organization that I have worked, there has been someone there who becomes the "therapist" in the group—the person who spends much of his/her time coaching others on how to get their job done and how to get promoted. Sometimes it's a human resources professional (hopefully), or sometimes just someone who is a strong mentor and takes these things seriously. He/she lives to help others in the workplace.

The Party Animal

You know this person! Every waking (and probably non-waking) moment is about the next social get-together. Every business trip has a social element to it; every business meeting is about where to go out for drinks that night. The party animal's question is always, "Where's the party in this proposal?"

The Perfect Parents

The people who all their life just wanted to have a family. They geared their education, their dating, and their career choices around getting ready for children. Now that they have them, they devote all of their time toward their well-being. They work hard for their family, and they love every minute of it. This might be the high school gym teacher who also coaches, or the work-at-home small business owner who has made career choices so that he can be with his family.

I have certainly been there, done that.

Are these stereotypes?

Yes, I suppose, but they are meant to just illustrate a point. What they really show is that through consistent behavior and deliberate choices, people become brands. You know who they are, and you probably can anticipate what they are going to do in any given situation.

Based on the choices they have made in their lives and their current situation, we can be pretty sure where their lives will be going from here on out. For some of these folks, this was all a deliberate plan, and for others, they just sort of fell into it. Either way, I hope you can see that they have started to form their own personal brand.

A few more examples, a little more real and a lot more famous, that will help put a face to this concept of *The Personal Experience Effect*:

Meryl Streep

The quintessential American actress. Career longevity like no other. With decades in the business, year after year still churning out blockbuster hits and critical acclaims she has performed a wide variety of roles and has not had a lick of tabloid scandal. She is apparently starting to mentor the next generation in Anne Hathaway, which is also a sign of a good brand—establishing a legacy!

Lady Gaga

She is new to the scene but is clearly establishing who she is as a hyper-creative artist. She creates pulsing beats, infectious lyrics, and outlandish costumes, but she is all about the underdog. She is musically centered but cultivates partnerships with brands like MAC cosmetics and Polaroid, which is also the sign of a powerful brand.

Anderson Cooper

The longest overnight success in journalism. On the ground for all the big worldwide news stories (like the devastation in New Orleans and in Haiti), he has created a reputation for telling us exactly what is happening at the moment, from the middle of the scene. Anderson Cooper has established his brand consistently, whether it's on air or online in his blog, Twitter account, or Facebook page.

Steve Jobs (one of my personal favorites)

The ultimate visionary and innovator, who created products that radically changed our lives. Without a doubt, the one business CEO who had the biggest impact on my personal life even though we sadly never met. His work keeps me connected every single day of my life.

These are perfect portrayals of people who know who they are and have made great choices in their lives, establishing themselves as great brands in their fields.

Each of them has (seemingly deliberately) created his/her own *Personal Experience Effect* and has risen to the pinnacles of his/her profession. If you notice, though, none of them has had a picture perfect life, yet all of them have created a legacy for others to follow or have picked up a legacy from those before them.

Lady Gaga was inspired by so many, including Donna Summer and Madonna, for example. Future entertainment brands will soon say that they were inspired by Lady Gaga.

The point here is that Meryl Streep, Lady Gaga, and Anderson Cooper have become brands just like Tide, Apple, and J.Crew

As are you!

That's right, you can do this too, and you probably have already gotten a good start. You just need to make it more of a conscious process so that you can steer your life toward what you want to accomplish.

You need an outline for a personal marketing plan, just like a brand does.

Brand managers follow a very rigorous process to determine their marketing plan, and they update it every single year. Trust me, I've done it over and over again through the years in virtually every consumer category you can think of, for the biggest brands in the world. It's a deliberate process, but it's also very creative (or certainly should be).

Although this process was built for the big brands, like Colgate, it can be easily applied to people, and that's what we're doing right here.

The result of all that planning will be a roadmap for getting what you want out of life and, ultimately, a reputation that serves you well.

Both personally and professionally, you'll have your own brand and your very own *Personal Experience Effect*.

As you read through this book, I will show you the way, much like I coach and consult brand managers on how to market their brands and get what they want for their businesses. It's really the same, except now it's about you!

I start out the book in chapter one by talking more about *The Personal Experience Effect* in terms of what it really means and what it really does for you.

Then in chapter two, we will get started by defining who you want to be as a person. It's an important first step, and we can't move ahead without knowing what we want out of life. Every brand does it, and so should you.

In chapter three, we will apply that brand definition into two classic marketing concepts: a positioning statement and an elevator pitch. Don't know what those are? Not only will you know them, you will have them for your brand.

Chapter four is where we explore the choices we make in life. Marketing is all about making good choices, so we will examine how the choices you make form who you are and who you want to be. Your consistent choices will form your brand, so you need to do it consciously, every step of the way.

Chapter five covers understanding your audience. Just like a brand, you need to understand the wants and needs of those around you, or of those who you want to have around you. It's the friends, family, and coworkers who surround you who perceive your behavior and, ultimately, create your brand. It's important to know what they want so that you can create the right kind of brand for yourself and for them.

Chapter six is where we construct our marketing plan, just as if we were a big global brand. We will construct a plan just as I have advised my clients through the years—from Tylenol to Kellogg's to Ambien to Paul Mitchell. Once you know what you want, you can more easily write out the plan to get there, and that's exactly what we will do.

In chapter seven, we will hit the crux of *The Personal Experience Effect* where we talk about consistency. For a brand to resonate with its consumers, it must behave consciously and consistently each and every time. So too must you if you want to be a brand.

Chapter eight dives into identifying what you need to become your brand. You are probably on your way, but there are always more things to do. Good marketing is never complete, and neither are we as people. We'll figure out what's missing from our branding and how to fill in the gaps.

Chapter nine looks into being flexible. Life throws us many curveballs. We need to have a personal marketing plan that is flexible enough to respond to the changes that happen in life. Plus we can always exercise the option to change our minds!

Chapter ten goes online. The digital world has made this both easier and harder at the same time. I see it with my teenage kids whose entire lives are online and on display. The choices we make are now all up for public sharing and evaluation, making the creation of a brand even more important. We'll explore how to navigate the entire online world and how to manage your brand properly in the process.

Chapter eleven covers your brand's look and voice. It's important to look and sound the part—in this case, the part is your brand.

Chapter twelve takes your brand to the market—for finding a job, for a new date, for family, or for whatever your life takes you. It's time to put your great branding to use.

Chapter thirteen is about those around you who support your brand. You should surround yourself with those who will help you achieve your goals.

Finally, chapter fourteen explores adding some purpose to your brand and talks about how you can give back to those in need—in your community, to the next generation, or for whatever fits your brand.

Throughout this book, I will bring in a lot of examples from other brands to help illustrate each point. I believe strongly that we can learn a lot by observing brands in action. It's a part of my own branding, that's for sure. One of my brand themes is "Marketing is a Spectator Sport," and I plan to prove that throughout each topic.

As you read this book, feel free to visit my website: http://JimJosephExp.com. It's where you will find my take on the great brands around us, and hopefully, you will find inspiration for what you are trying to build. You can also meet one another.

You'll also get to see more of my brand.

I love marketing, and I am honored that I can bring the principles of good marketing that I have learned throughout my entire career to you. Hopefully, it will help you build your own brand so that you can get what you want out of life.

The Personal Experience Effect.

Good luck to you and to your brand. Enjoy the process.

1 Learn
The Experience Effect

You may not ever have thought about yourself as being in marketing, but the truth is that when it comes to your own life, you are in fact a marketer—a marketer of yourself.

Marketing can mean a lot of things to a lot of people, so let's put a definition around it.

I've gone through most of my career with a pretty clear picture of marketing, and in fact, for the most part, I considered it to be somewhat simple to understand. Perhaps not so easy to execute, but somewhat easy to at least understand what it's all about.

Boy, did I get a little surprise from an unlikely place.

One of the LinkedIn groups I joined put out a challenge question: "How do you define marketing?" At first glance, I thought it was the craziest thing I have ever heard. "What a stupid question," I said right out loud. "Everyone will give the same answer."

(By the way if you're managing a career, and you have not joined LinkedIn, then put this book down right now and go join. It'll do wonders for the professional side of your brand, which we will talk about later.)

Well, several months later, the debate was still raging, as different members from different industries offered their own definition of marketing. I finally had to turn off the comments because the arguments were starting to make me dizzy.

It made me realize, though, that there are many dimensions to marketing, and most everyone was right in his/her own interpretation. There were a few bizarre ideas in the mix, but for the most part, each definition fit the bill for that person.

Marketing is an art that has many subtleties, even for the big brands. As clear-cut as it might seem from the outside for a brand like Starbucks, there are so many nuances to be managed. It takes an entire team of employees and agencies to get it all done correctly and seamlessly.

But that's Starbucks.

When it comes to marketing ourselves, there's no reason why we can't apply some of those big brand principles to ourselves. We can make marketing personal, so to speak.

With personal branding, marketing is how you serve yourself up to those around you and what you consistently offer to them. Said another way, personal marketing is basically making sure that you give people what they want, in order to ultimately get what you want.

I realize that I just turned it around on you, so let's look at a big brand example like Tide.

When it comes to a brand like Tide, the branding and the marketing is all about what it can do for its consumers—in this case, giving people ways to clean their family's clothes. The Tide brand gives its consumers something of benefit to them so that they will buy it over and over. The brand provides a good, consistent product in order to get consumer loyalty.

When it comes to yourself, in a similar manner, you give other people something so that you can get something back in return. Allow me to explain.

At work, you complete projects so that you can get a paycheck. In your personal life, you provide friendship so that you get friendship in return. In each case, you give so that you can receive.

The work you do and the friendships you provide are an experience that you offer to others. It's the experience that they receive that is a benefit to them. When marketing yourself, it's about consciously building that experience so that you can effectively get what you want in return.

That's how I answered that LinkedIn question: marketing is all about creating a consistent experience for your customers. This is true whether you are a person or a business.

For you, it's about creating an experience for those around you so that you can be successful both personally and professionally. In essence, that is your *Personal Experience Effect*—it's the experience you offer others so that you can get what you want in return. You provide an experience and receive a benefit in return.

One of my favorite examples from music history is Donna Summer, the Queen of Disco. You can't say her name without saying her tagline. It's impossible. Then images of disco balls and dancing at clubs immediately pop into our heads.

Donna Summer was a brand that was clearly created and defined at the time to give people what they want, and she sold millions of records in return. Donna Summer was an experience, and for those of you old enough to have enjoyed it, then you know what I mean!

It worked brilliantly for Donna Summer, and it sounds quite simple on the surface: you provide a personal brand experience for others, and then hopefully you get a positive effect from it—the more positive the experience, then, obviously, the more effective the result.

Of course, you want your brand experience to be exactly the way you want it to be. You need it to be purposeful, and that takes some thinking and some planning, which isn't always so simple. Your personal brand should be a reflection of who you want to be, and the experience you offer people should match that, which is a lot of work.

This wasn't always true for Donna Summer, if you know her story, which is why she felt conflicted about her own brand. As a result, her longevity and brand didn't sustain for as long as her potential would have indicated. She couldn't stay consistent to the brand she had created, so it faded too quickly. But when the sun was on her, boy, was she a sensation!

The lesson learned there is that you have to take control. You are your own brand manager, and you have to set the course for your own brand experience. It's your show.

We will be spending the rest of our time in this book talking about how to make the decisions necessary to build the right kind of experience for your personal brand, so that you can in fact get what you want out of life. It's up to you to create the exact brand experience to get exactly what you want out of your life.

Your brand experience becomes who you are and how you live your life. It determines how people perceive you, whether you intend it or not. You need to make it intentional.

I know for me, through the years, I have very carefully crafted what I think my brand is all about both personally and professionally. I know who I am (and who I am not), and I know what I want out of life. When I hit a crossroads, I lean on my brand to help me make a good decision based on what I've decided that I want it to be.

While I am a person, I am certainly also a brand, and I market myself very consciously, which is something that I have learned to do over the years. It didn't come automatically for sure. I have my own very *Personal Experience Effect*, and I live it every day.

I am a marketer of my own brand experience.

You need to do the same. You need to consciously create your brand experience to get the effect you want out of life.

The Personal Experience Effect. It will affect your success, both personally and professionally.

You may not have realized it before, but in this sense, you are both a brand and a marketer. Welcome aboard.

Let's get started.

NOTES

2 Create Who You Want to Be

J. K. Rowling: Fantastic Creator of Characters

Ready?

We are going to start the process just like we would with a big brand—the way virtually every marketing brand manager does almost every single year.

To get us going, we will start by asking ourselves, "What would Nike do?"

In this case, I really can answer that question because I've worked on many big brands in my career, and there are definitely some common patterns across them all.

Now I have never worked on Nike (although that would be a dream client), but I've managed many on the same scale and global caliber. I can tell you with confidence that most start out in a very similar manner: by creating a brand definition.

They all start out by defining their brand.

When scoping out their business models and marketing plans, all the big brands start with an outline of what their brand is all about. The brand managers do an analysis of the kinds of things that the brand is particularly good at and the kind of things that they want the brand to develop. Big brands pull together an inventory of skills that could possibly make them who they are, and they construct it into a brand definition.

They define their brand!

It's a critical first step in building your *Personal Experience Effect* and arguably the most important. Without a proper definition of your personal brand, we can't possibly market it.

Part of that process is also indentifying how the brand can be unique from others in the same space, and how to build a unique experience unlike all others around you. But we'll get to that later.

Back to Nike.

So as Nike originally defined its brand as "sports gear for the weekend warrior" (or something like that), they must have realized that they have core capabilities in sports gear design, manufacturing, and distribution—or they at least have the knowledge to figure out how to get there. I'm sure the brand also determined that they could create something unique in the marketplace with these skills, something that would set them apart from their competitors like Reebok or Adidas. They also must have determined that they could be quite successful at it.

You need to do the same for your personal brand:

- Identify your skills and attributes (the ones you have now or the ones you want to have).

- Make sure you can excel at them.

- Determine if you can make them unique.

- Understand if they will bring you success and happiness.

Sounds simple, right?

Start your thinking by outlining all the areas of your life where you want to achieve success and happiness. This would also include your social life, relationships, children, and places where you want to live. It's so easy to just focus on your career; even though that might be a huge part, it shouldn't be the sole area of development.

You want your brand to be well-rounded and to capture all aspects of your life.

Begin to outline all the aspects of your life that you want as part of your brand definition. Start with some pretty basic questions to get you into the swing of it, including the importance of:

- continued education

- a career that occupies your life

- children (when and how many)

- a monogamous relationship

- being a player in the dating world

- friends

- your own home

- living in the city vs. the country

These are just some of the aspects of your life that you'll want to roll into your brand definition.

Chapter 2: Create Who You Want to Be

Remember that your brand definition should be aspirational: an indication of what you want out of life, not necessarily where you are right now.

When I think of these types of things, I tend to think of how authors create characters. Think about J. K. Rowling and her *Harry Potter* series. She created these fantastic, magical characters that were either already well-defined brands in their lives or were just beginning to get their lives in order. J. K. Rowling created character brands that represented a spectrum of life experiences, personalities, and motivations.

Each character had a specific role in the story and a specific mission in life.

As for me, I've always considered myself to be a NYer (as in Manhattan). It has always been a part of my brand long before I ever lived there, and I'm not sure that I can even tell you why. I grew up in Upstate New York but still identified myself with Manhattan. I went to grad school at Columbia but, believe it or not, didn't actually live in Manhattan until I was thirty-nine!

But I've always been a NYer and always will be. I even ran the New York City Marathon to add that experience to my brand. I wanted to be a true New Yorker.

Funny thing is that now all we hear is "Brooklyn is the new Manhattan," so I have to adjust my brand thinking. I'm not there yet, but it's on my radar and may hit my brand plan!

I also see myself as a global CEO of a multinational company and, honestly, always have. I'm not there yet by any means, but I'm hopefully on my way! It's definitely in my brand plan. If you don't have these kinds of goals and can't visualize them, then they will never happen.

If these kinds of aspirations are a core part of who you think you are and who you want to be, then you need to build them into your brand definition right from the start.

Me? Well, I'm a global CEO based out of Manhattan, thank you very much! (Or at least I will be someday.) I love building and fixing organizations that are based on the craft of marketing. I take great delight in solving business problems.

I also always saw myself as a dad, and it was that desire that guided many of my early life decisions, both personally and certainly professionally. I basically started my own agency so that I could take care of my children, so that I could be home and around for them.

These important elements of my brand are driving decisions that I needed to make every day. Many of those decisions have since changed through the years, but that's another book.

I have two amazing children, who are almost adults now, who are still a huge part of my brand definition. I wouldn't be Jim Joseph, and I wouldn't want to be Jim Joseph, without "dad" being a part of my brand definition.

Having a steady, consistent, stable relationship has always been important to me as well, in addition to a network of friends. Knowing that, I put a lot of effort into finding a life partner. It took me awhile, that's for sure, but I got there. And I have many of the same friends and colleagues whom I've had for decades, thanks in part to Facebook!

My relationships go from grade school to college to all of my jobs. My friends are the relationships that help to define my brand, in addition of course to my partner and children.

When you start to pull that together, you can start to get a pretty good definition of the Jim Joseph brand. You can and should absolutely do the same.

Pulling me together, you'll see that I'm a married Manhattanite with children, who runs a global company, thriving within a huge social network of friends and colleagues.

My brand definition is not completely there yet, but I'm on my way.

As the years have gone by, different aspects of my brand definition have taken priority. It was more about the kids when they were young, not as much now with them both in college.

As social media has grown in importance, the social networking aspect of my brand has been taking more priority, and that's a lot of fun.

Are you starting to get a sense of my brand and how I've defined it? Can you see how you could do the same with your brand definition?

Of course this is just a start; we need to go much deeper and add more meaning to it. We need to turn this into a *positioning* for your brand to make this even more useful.

Shall we?

NOTES

3 Position Yourself

Meryl Streep: The Most Decorated American Actor

Fasten your seatbelts, because now we're getting to the good stuff.

Positioning.

I've written quite a bit about positioning in my books and blog posts. I believe that positioning is one of the most misunderstood parts of marketing, and quite honestly, most people get it completely wrong. In fact, many very experienced people in marketing get it wrong a lot of the time. But you're going to get it right for your *Personal Experience Effect*!

Positioning is a natural next step from your brand definition because it's a summation of all the attributes you've selected for your brand.

A positioning statement brings them all together, without any of the detail, to become a guidepost for how people will think about your brand and for how you will guide it through the years.

Let's first talk about what *positioning* exactly is.

Most people overcomplicate it in an attempt to understand it. My approach: simplify to make it actionable.

I'm going to keep it super simple with a street-smart definition of positioning: positioning is the space you want to occupy in your target audience's mind when they think of you.

- Positioning is not a statement about you; it's a statement that captures you.

- Positioning is not the facts about what you do; it's a summary of the effect you have.

- Positioning is not a factual claim; it's the emotional reason why people want to be around you.

- Positioning should capture the essence of who you are and how you have defined your personal brand; it's how people should think about you, when they think about you.

Let's look at a big brand example again: Nike.

The positioning of Nike isn't "sports gear." "Sports gear" is a statement about the Nike brand; it's what the Nike brand does, and it's more of a claim. It's not a positioning statement.

The Nike positioning statement would be something more like, "Lets me feel and perform like an athlete."

See what I mean? This statement is much more emotional and much more about how people feel for and think about the Nike brand.

The positioning of Nike is how the brand wants you to think of it when you think of it. Then, of course, it's a marketer's job to get you to think about the brand more often!

Take a look at Meryl Streep, America's most decorated actor.

She has a very clear definition of her brand—an actress who completely transforms herself in every role she takes on, whether dramatic, comedic, or something in between. Whether set in contemporary situations or reinventing historical moments. She's an actress with deep skills in taking her audience to new places, to experience a slice of someone else's life. Meryl Streep's brand is very well-defined.

So, too, can be yours.

Take your personal attributes that you outlined and create a positioning statement that captures the essence of who you are. Write a positioning statement that says how you want people to think and feel about you.

You may need a few dimensions to it in order to capture the various facets of your life. A positioning statement that describes your professional aspirations may not cover all parts of your home life and vice versa. You need to capture your total brand.

I long ago came up with my own positioning statement, mostly at work. I didn't even realize that is what I was doing!

I think it was from years of doing interviews when I would ask people to tell me about themselves. These folks, fifteen minutes and quite a few yawns later, would still be talking about themselves. And I wouldn't remember a single thing.

Many people would just drone on and on about their lives, with no purpose for me to take away. They gave me a laundry list of facts about themselves, without any sense of describing who they actually were.

I vowed never to do that myself.

A positioning statement can help you give a concise answer to that oh-so-standard interview question.

I have built my career either launching or rebuilding brands and agencies. I've been a marketer on both sides of the client/agency fence, and in my first job at Johnson & Johnson, I became a bit of a new products expert.

So when I'm in a professional setting and people ask me to tell them about myself, I say, 'I'm a builder and a fixer of organizations and their brands."

It instantly answers the question yet opens the door for them to sincerely and interestingly ask for more information. It doesn't divulge my whole story all at once but rather sets up an intriguing dialogue where I can hit the highlights in my career.

It then allows me to weave in other aspects of my life—like being able to build my career while also raising two children and guiding them in their lives.

Now if I am out with friends, I don't necessarily say that I'm a "builder and fixer," although you could say that I build networks of friends and colleagues who help one another. See, there you go, a positioning statement that works in multiple settings.

A positioning statement is so much more effective than a long story about every career move I have made. It intrigues people and leaves them wanting more. It doesn't bore them or make them wish that they had never asked.

It draws them into my brand.

Notice, too, that it's got a bit of emotion in it. You can feel a little something about me when you hear my positioning statement.

Clearly the positioning statement doesn't answer all of the questions, but it does start the process.

Next comes the elevator pitch.

The elevator pitch is a quick extension of the positioning statement that provides a little more detail. The term *elevator pitch* comes from the notion that you should be able to tell your story in the length of time it takes to ride in an elevator. Granted, it might be a tall building, but you need to make it quick and efficient. If you haven't convinced someone in that amount of time, you're never going to convince them at all.

They will tune you out.

Think in quick sound bytes or Twitter posts. A few comments that tie together your story and make your positioning statement come to life.

Me? I'm a builder and a fixer of organizations and their brands.

I started my career in classic brand management at Johnson & Johnson and became a new products expert. I started my own agency that I quickly sold, merging together several small agencies to create an integrated marketing company—the largest of its kind in Manhattan at the time.

I've reinvented various kinds of traditional agencies and have brought them thriving into the world of integrated marketing.

Ding! We've arrived at my floor!

My elevator pitch is short, to the point, and laddering up to and completing my positioning statement.

Again, I've focused this on the career side of my life, assuming for the purposes here that I'm in an interview situation. Bringing up my children and all of the decisions that I've made to support them wouldn't necessarily be the first priority or the first part of my brand that I would highlight.

But I could easily and quickly add in those layers. The reason why I started my own agency was because I had two children both under four, and I needed to be home to take care of them. As they got older, I was then able to get more and more diverse with my career, which is how I ended up in Manhattan, running some of the world's largest agencies.

I've had the support of a caring partner every step of the way.

I've been a builder and fixer of my family's lives as well, including my own!

Can you see how my elevator pitch brings dimension to my positioning statement and gives detail to my brand definition?

Now it's time for you to craft your brand definition, positioning statement, and elevator pitch. You'll need it to build your *Personal Experience Effect.*

Outline here the main attributes that make up your brand definition, now and in the future.

1.

2.

3.

4.

5.

6.

How could you then summarize that in a positioning statement?

And then list out, in short form, the accomplishments you've made that could become your elevator pitch.

1.

2.

3.

4.

Now you're ready to put these brand elements to good use in building your *Personal Experience Effect.*

NOTES

4 Make Good Choices

James Carville: Democratic Strategist

If you read any of my blog posts, you know that I always say that a marketer's job is all about making good decisions. This is probably true of any occupation, but it is certainly true when it comes to brand management.

Brand managers are really just decision makers in disguise.

Many don't realize it, but most marketers spend the bulk of their day making decisions. They review pricing analyses, look at distribution reports, think through changes in packaging design, complete product taste tests—an entire range of marketing activities that all require a decision.

There's actually no disguising that because it's the marketers' job to make those decisions. Sometimes they have thorough data in hand, and other times they have to make decisions on the fly and trust their gut.

No matter the situation, though, they need something to guide them.

So far you've made some pretty critical decisions as part of chapter two when it came to defining your personal brand and developing your positioning. See? You're already a marketer!

These are the exact tools that marketers use to guide their decisions as well. They have a brand definition, and they have a fully developed brand positioning statement that they put into action on a regular basis. So anytime they are faced with a decision, they benchmark against their goals, their brand definition, and their brand positioning. Every decision is determined against those measuring sticks.

The key is for you to do the same from now on.

Let's look at some of the big commercial brands. Take Martha Stewart, the brand.

I always use Martha Stewart in my NYU class as a classic example of a brand and its decisions. There's no arguing that Martha Stewart, the brand, is a mega-success. Her legions of fans attest to that, as do her multiple product lines across various retail outlets and partnerships. Her brand stretches far and wide and has been very successful. You can't take that away from her, no matter your perspective.

The Martha Stewart brand has not always been successful at every turn, though. It has certainly had some amazing successes, based on some really good decisions, like the network television show, the many books, and the collaboration with Kmart, just to name a few.

But Martha Stewart the brand has made some not-so-good decisions as well, professionally speaking. Her television show *The Apprentice*, while on paper probably seemed like a good idea, damaged her brand terribly. Not only did it bomb in the ratings, it tarnished her image and set her brand back. It was not a wise decision, in hindsight, to portray her brand in that manner.

The brand has also done a "buffet" of partnerships with so many retailers, some of whom have worked well and others whom have not. Each and every one of them was a key decision made by the brand managers, which presumably were tied to how they define the Martha Stewart brand.

We've also been public witnesses to some decisions that Martha Stewart has made in her personal life, which were not necessarily good for the brand either. It's testament to the fact that when a person is tied to the equity of a brand, then that person's decisions affect the brand as well, often in a very damaging way.

In a similar fashion, the decisions you make will undoubtedly affect your personal brand and either contribute to or damage your *Personal Experience Effect*.

We talked about Meryl Streep in the last chapter. Now there's a personal brand that has made a lot of good decisions. Every role she accepts is a decision based on her brand definition and her goals. Almost flawless.

James Carville, democratic strategist, is another great example of a personal brand who has consistently made amazingly good decisions.

Whether you agree with the politics or not, you have to acknowledge that the man has carved out a unique brand for himself, with his unique skill sets. There are not that many others like him, and he clearly differentiates himself from the pack.

James Carville has made great decisions along his career to move from various political posts, to analyst positions, to the media spotlight. He calls himself a *democratic strategist*, and he is at the top of this game because of the consistent decisions he has made in his life—consistent with his brand definition and with his goals.

Interesting to note that his wife, Mary Matalin, is also a brand on the other side of the fence—as a Republican. I find it fascinating to see their two brands coexist; it shows the power of branding. They have even coauthored a successful book.

When assembling your personal brand, learn from these great brands and the people behind them by watching how they make decisions about their brands, their personal lives, and their careers. The really successful brands are incredibly consistent. Brands that stray off strategy, as marketers would say, get themselves in trouble because their audience can't process the inconsistency.

Take a look at Tiger Woods. Sure, it was awful that he was having so many affairs all around the country. He made some horrible choices for his brand and his family. The worst part about it was the inconsistency.

Imagine if had Tiger been single. He would have been applauded for being a "player." His indiscretions all around the country would have been inspiration for the single guy, and there would have been many women who would have found it sexy.

But that's not how Tiger had served himself up to us. He seemed quiet, a family man who focused on his career and provided everything to his wife and family.

The sudden news of different kinds of behavior was shocking. He clearly made the wrong decisions based on who he was as a brand. And his brand, and those other brands around him, suffered greatly. We didn't know how to process it all, so many dropped his brand as a result.

Take a lesson here.

The same could be said of you as you manage your personal brand. Each and every choice you make should reinforce your positioning. Collectively, the choices you make throughout your life help to either reinforce your brand or detract from it. If you don't like the choices you are making, then you need to either make new ones, or you need to change your brand.

If Tiger Woods liked the choices he was making, then he needed to change his brand to better reflect those choices. Or else he needed to change his choices despite himself.

Use the tools you have developed so far—that's why they are here! Your brand positioning should be your guide to how you manage your brand and how you make decisions. If you hold your brand positioning up each and every time, you are much more likely to do the right thing for your personal brand.

Hopefully, you'll also be much more likely to do what's right for your life.

NOTES

5 Understand Your Audience

Jillian Michaels: Television's Toughest Trainer

One of the fundamental truths of good marketing is making sure you understand your audience—not only who they are but also what makes them tick.

Marketers spend an enormous amount of time, energy, and money on identifying who is best suited for their brand, and then how to best build their brand experience to suit them. Figuring out who is *best suited* is something we call determining the *target market*.

In other words, "Who should we target to buy our brand?"

The same could be said for your personal brand.

It's important to understand who your audience is if you really want your personal brand to be successful.

In this case, we are going to have several audiences, based on the various parts of our lives. We will need to target our audiences or, in other words, the people in our personal, social, and professional lives.

You must ask yourself a fundamental question in each and every case: "What do these people want from me that can in turn help me to be successful?" Notice the order of that question.

First: What do these people want from me

Then: that can help me be successful?

Any good marketer puts his target audience first.

The success of your personal brand depends, in large part, on how others perceive you and how satisfied they are with their experiences with you. Now they don't talk about it this way, but this is the net effect.

This is *The Personal Experience Effect*.

So in each and every case, you need to think about how to please your audience first, and then your personal brand will soar.

This is certainly true at work.

When you put your boss's needs first, then you will shine at the right time.

When you put your coworkers' needs first, then they will help you in return.

When you put your team's needs first, then they will help you get projects done.

Then and only then will your brand be successful, whatever your professional goals are. The same is true of your personal and social life.

When you put your family's needs first, they will grow to love you even more.

When you put your friends' needs first, then they will do the same in return.

Then and only then will your brand be successful both personally and professionally.

Now, of course, you can't please everyone all the time; that's impossible, and I'm not implying that this should be your goal. Your goal should be personal success created by having those around you feel good about being around you.

Prioritize those that will help you get there sooner.

If your goal is to marry and have children, then surround yourself with people who can help you get there. Make them happy to be around you, and they will connect you to others.

If your goal is to become a renowned writer, then surround yourself with people who can help you get there. Make them happy, and they will connect you to others.

If your goal is to have a big network of friends, then go for it. Make them all happy to be around you, and they will do the heavy lifting and will connect you to others.

If you are not currently surrounded by people who can do this for you, then I would argue one of two things:

- You've defined your brand incorrectly, and you are, therefore, not treating people appropriately.

- You've surrounded yourself with the wrong people.

If neither one of those things is true, then you are not doing the right things for your personal brand. Do more to fulfill their needs, and they will do more to make you successful regardless of your goal.

That's what the big brands do.

The big brands make their audiences very happy, in an effort to build brand loyalty. They introduce new products, distribute coupons, and create Facebook pages—all with the goal of making their target market happy. The big brands give and give and give, hoping for sales in return.

Look at Jillian Michaels, television's toughest trainer who got her start on the big brand *The Biggest Loser*.

This woman knows her audience, and in fact, it's her audience that built her brand. She targets those who need tough love, and she uniquely delivers it. She inspires those with tough weight loss and health goals and who have a tough road ahead of them. Her toughness will push them through the barriers that will definitely get in the way.

She's tough, and she surrounds herself with those who like it and need it that way. In return, they have made her brand successful.

Tough, tough, tough. Notice the consistency and the link to delivering to her audience.

You simply need to do the same with your target market.

For example, if part of your brand is to be a connoisseur of fine dining and food/wine pairings, then, first and foremost, you need to include that as part of your brand definition. Then you need to make it a part of the experience of being with you and offer that as a benefit to your audience, and they will give you other things in return.

Of course, you need to understand your audience. Hanging around with a lot of people who eat fast food and drink beer at the local bar isn't going to work with the brand definition above. So you need to either change your brand or change your audience or, at a minimum, find other ways to connect with them that interests you.

Think of it this way: surround yourself with people, both socially and professionally, who want to share your brand experience with you. Perhaps even surround yourself with those who know more about the experience than you do.

This should inspire you.

If having a graduate diploma is part of your brand definition, then surround yourself with those who have it or know how to get it. Make them thrilled to be around you, happy in the knowledge that they are helping to build your brand, whether they realize it or not.

This is your target market, and you need to embrace it. Get to know what they want, and they will give you what you want in return.

As you develop your personal brand and the experience that comes along with it, you must ask yourself one question: who's my audience?

NOTES

6 Make a Plan

Julia Child: America's First French Chef

All of this discussion has been well and good, but it's all for nothing if we don't put it into action. This is where the rubber meets the road, and you become a marketer of your personal brand.

If you were doing this for a living on a national brand, the notion of developing a marketing plan would be second nature to you. Those of us who have managed brands are very much used to writing an annual plan for our businesses.

Every year, usually at the end of the summer, we as marketers carve out what we want to accomplish on the brand in the next year—how we are going to do it all and how much it will likely cost. And then we map out a course of action for each item we need to get done in order to hit those goals.

We do this on an annual basis, but we also keep a rolling plan for one year, three years, five years, and ten years out. I'm doing it today for our clients.

You should do the same if you want to build your brand and your own *Personal Experience Effect.*

Let's start in a simple place (ha!) and write out our goals—goals for the next ten years, five, three, and then one year. It may sound obvious, but you need to know where you want to go before you can plan how to get there.

Some of this you've had to do in order to develop your brand definition and positioning statement. You need a sense of who you want to be—what you want your personal brand to be—in order to define it and position it.

It makes sense, right?

But now that you are going to plan out your brand, you need to be more specific about your goals. What do you want to accomplish, both personally and professionally, over the course of the next few years? What do you want, both short-term and long-term?

It may seem obvious, but not always easy.

Do you want to have children?

Do you want a life partner?

Where do you want to live and raise a family?

Are friends important to you, or are you more of a solo artist?

When it comes to work, do you want to be in a large organization?

Do you aspire to be a senior manager or more of a worker?

Do you want to be in a creative field, or something more analytical?

You have to carve out goals that are in keeping with the brand definition you have spelled out. As you are mapping out your goals, ask yourself: does this work with my positioning statement and with what I want my elevator pitch to be?

You've already done some of the hard thinking, so make sure that everything matches up to that.

Think of your goals as a rolling weather forecast.

Start with what you want ten years from now, and then work backward. You could go even farther out, but it gets kind of difficult to think too far ahead. I think it's easier to think in ten-year increments, but that's just me!

It's a classic interview question, although now it has increased importance: where do you want to be in ten years?

From there you can map out an interim five-year goal and then an even closer three-year goal and so on.

Take a look at personal brand Julia Child, America's first French chef.

Her path led to being a television and pop culture icon, but it didn't happen overnight. While she was living in France, she took cooking classes at a famous school to learn French techniques. She then wrote a book that became a classic, leading to a career in teaching on television.

I've oversimplified it here, but the point is that Julia Child defined her brand, decided what she wanted, and then planned out how to get there.

Some of it was completely intentional, and some just rolled out along the way. We will talk later about being flexible through the process. Either way, take some inspiration from the brand Julia Child and her plan to become what I would call a pop culture icon.

Me?

I'm no Julia Child (nor do I cook much), but I always knew I wanted to be in marketing. Not sure why, but I just did. Somehow, someone told me that in order to do that, I needed to get an MBA. In order to get an MBA, I needed some good business experience coming out of college. In order to get some good business experience, I needed a good college education.

See how it all flows? One accomplishment flows into the other, which is why it takes a plan to map it all out.

So as a junior in high school, I set my sights on Cornell University for my undergraduate program because I liked the business program there, and the college environment there just fit me at the time.

After graduation, I worked for two years in sales at Carnation (which is now Nestle). I left Nestle to go to Columbia University, where I got my MBA in marketing and finance. I majored in both marketing and finance because I knew that marketing people are also responsible for brand sales and profits, so I needed to be comfortable working financial sheets.

While at school, I did a summer internship at Johnson & Johnson, in the baby products division. As soon as I finished my MBA, I rushed right back to J&J to be an assistant product director, and a marketer was born, ten years in the making.

It was a ten-year process of goal setting, making interim goal steps along the way. Of course, being an assistant product director at J&J wasn't my end goal, but more of a milestone in my long-term plans. I wanted to move up into the ranks of management, get experience on all sides of the marketing equation, write a book or two, and, eventually, teach the craft.

I'm still a work in progress along my plan; it's just that the ten-year horizons have shifted through the years.

It's been a rolling process of goal setting all along the way. What's next for me? If you read my marketing plan, you would know!

I couldn't possibly wake up one day and say that I want to write a book and teach. Anyone who does that has to build at least a little credibility on the topic, and that takes years of planning and experience.

Remember my positioning statement: "I'm a builder and a fixer."

I started out building brands and fixing agencies. Although I continue to do that, I also build young careers through my books and teaching. See, I've tried to be incredibly consistent and always tie my goals to my brand definition and positioning statement.

As I progress through my career, my elevator pitch about my skills and accomplishments starts to paint a story.

We've only been talking about my career here, not my personal life. You'll want to look at all aspects of your life when you set your goals. I knew that I always wanted to be a dad, and I also knew that I always wanted someone (just one someone) to share my life. I made decisions and set goals along the way. Now that my kids are off to college, we are setting new goals about the next ten years.

I am fortunate to say that I have felt successful all along the way, despite the bumps and curves.

Now it's time for you to have some fun! Here's a little chart to help you map out your goals and, ultimately, your ten-year plan. Fill it out and you'll feel like you are well on your way to achieving what you want out of life.

Start now.

My Personal 10-Year Plan

Action Plan

Goal	1-Year	3-Year	5-Year	10-Year

NOTES

7 Ensure Consistency

Abraham Lincoln: Civil Rights Innovator

If there's one thing you should have picked up from the last chapter, it's the need to be consistent when it comes to personal branding. You won't be able to create a brand unless you are consistent—no one will know who you really are.

One of the key tenants of *The Personal Experience Effect* is that you be consciously consistent throughout your life—measured against your brand definition, your positioning, and then building toward your elevator pitch.

In some ways, it sounds rather obvious, I know, but in other ways, it feels virtually impossible. Think about your personal life and your friends, and I'm sure you know many people who are very consistent in what they do.

The person who is always there to help talk you out of a problem no matter what.

The person who always seems to be free to grab a drink with you.

The person who is always on time, no matter the circumstance.

The person you always invite to parties because he/she is always the life of the party.

The person at work who always gets projects done and, conversely, the other person who always fails to get projects done.

Always.

The person who never seems to be available without major advance notice.

The person who is never on time, so you plan accordingly.

The person who never talks about anything except himself/herself, no matter what you have going on in your life.

Never.

While these may seem like somewhat stereotypical character traits or personality features, they are consistent behaviors that shape a person and become one's brand. Importantly, they shape your perceptions of that person and, hence, your own behavior toward him/her.

I'm sure you act differently around each of those people that I just outlined, based on the consistency of their behavior.

Now what would happen if the person whom you can always count on suddenly doesn't respond to you anymore?

You make plans to meet him and he is horribly late.

Or he can't take your phone call this one time.

Or he is busy Friday night and can't meet you for a drink.

Or he is kind of quiet and aloof at the party.

Suddenly something's wrong. You don't know what to do. The person you thought you know so well is suddenly off-brand.

This happens to me quite a lot, I have to say.

I generally have a very upbeat, positive (dare I say), happy disposition. I like being around people, and I tend to be the cheerleader. Remember, I'm a builder and a fixer, which includes relationships and people's mood when they are around me. I can't help myself; it's my brand, and it comes quite naturally.

Well, it's hard to be that way all of the time. Sometimes I'm a little quieter than other times. Sometimes I'm really busy and focused. Sometimes I've been up too late the night before and am feeling a tired. I get up every day at 4:30 a.m. after all, and sometimes that youthful enthusiasm just doesn't last all day.

Not when you are "of a certain age!"

It's not that anything is wrong; quite the contrary—I'm totally fine. I just happen to not be as bubbly as usual. The problem, though, is that it sets people off. They don't know what to do. I'm not being my brand.

So I get questions:

"Are you mad at me?"

"Are you feeling okay today?"

"What's the matter?"

"What happened?"

And I get comments:

"You look tired."

"You seem different."

"You should go home."

Meanwhile, I am fine.

But I am off-brand that day, at least from their perspective. I'm not the Jim they rely on. I'm not consistent that day, so I am not delivering on my brand.

And it's not just my mood either.

I've developed a personal style with my clothes through the years that I think suits me. I like colorful shirts with fun patterns. I often wear jeans with a sports coat. I like to accessorize with scarves or hats. I guess I'm a clotheshorse to some extent.

It's not high fashion by any means, but I do take pride in having my own personal look to go with my personal brand. It's part of my *Personal Experience Effect.*

Now every once in a while, I purposely change it up, generally for a new business pitch or something like that. So I put a suit on. Or sometimes I'm feeling a little tired, and I throw on a flannel shirt and a really comfortable pair of jeans.

People don't like it.

In fact, they dislike it so much that they comment on it, especially when I'm wearing a suit. A suit for me, and from their perspective, is off-brand. It's inconsistent with what they associate with me. It throws them off, and I can honestly tell that they behave differently around me that day.

So I rarely wear a suit anymore, unless there is a specific business reason to do so. I know it all sounds weird, but that's the power of personal branding. That's literally *The Personal Experience Effect*.

We've noted consistency in behavior and clothing, but the principle applies to all aspects of your personal brand. Consistency is important in the choices you make throughout your life—in the way you approach relationships, how you do your work at work, etc.

You need to apply your brand consistently to each and every situation so that you can build your brand appropriately, and so that people know what to expect from you.

One of my favorite personal brands is Abraham Lincoln. Yes, that Abraham Lincoln.

Through the chronicles of history, a brand whom we know behaved very consistently. He effectively changed the course of history with his consistent policies and consistent point of view. You know that if he were alive today, he'd still be the same brand tackling the sociopolitical issues we currently debate. We can predict, based on his branc, what he'd be doing today.

You should be just as consistent.

You have a few tools in your back pocket to use to your advantage. Use your branc definition and positioning statement as guideposts.

I do it.

Every time I am in a difficult situation at work, I think of how my brand should behave.

For example, there are people we all encounter throughout our lives who are just impossible, and in fact, nobody can deal with them. But I am a builder and a fixer, so I always try to find a way to figure it out. I find something to connect with them. It's very purposefully my brand. And you know what? I have yet to find someone whom I can't work with.

That's because I know my brand: I'm a builder and a fixer, and I always find a way to create a connection.

People ask me all the time: "How do you get along with him?" I always figure out a way because that's my brand.

Always.

When I receive an off-color post on my Facebook page, I literally stop and ask myself how my brand should respond. I resist the temptation to say what I really want to make sure that I am on my brand—not in an artificial way but in a way that is all about who I am and who I want my brand to be.

I respond as Jim Joseph.

When I am at a party, depending on the party, I think through how I want my brand to be perceived. I have seen many people get himself/herself in trouble for not behaving on-brand at a party. Remember that every interaction makes up the totality of your brand, even those that seem to be just social.

Use your positioning as your guide for making decisions, and you will generally be consistent in your behavior and stay on your brand.

Consistently.

NOTES

Chapter

8 Know What You Need

Kim Kardashian: Branded Personality

I have said that all of this is a work in progress, so please don't get overwhelmed or intimidated. Take it one step at a time.

Your life is a journey, meant to be enjoyed along the way, while being yourself at every step. I'd like to think I'm a work in progress, hopefully trying new things every year that enhance my life and my brand. I just recently added "teaching a graduate level course at NYU" to my elevator pitch.

Hadn't done that before.

I'm sure that "President" is also just a step along the way for Barack Obama and his personal brand. I have a feeling that his journey is nowhere near its conclusion.

No matter where you are on your part of life, there's still more to come. I've seen many people in their sixties finally find their ultimate partner, knowing that being in a loving, compatible relationship was a part of their brand all along.

So if you are relatively early in your life and just figuring out what you want, don't be overwhelmed. Or if you've been around the block and still don't feel as if you've got it right, don't be frustrated.

This process of building *The Personal Experience Effect* is meant to make you more successful, but only when you do it step by step. Hold on tight to your aspirations, learn from the experiences along the way, and apply it to your personal brand. Oh, and have some fun, if it's a part of your brand.

This is not meant to get too corny or too much about self-actualization, but more about a message of hope. No one has it all figured out—I certainly don't, and almost everyone I know says the same.

Figuring out who you are and what you want out of life is an essential part of the process to get you there. Once you've got your brand definition set and your positioning statement in hand, it's time to figure out what you need to do and what you need to get in order to fulfill it.

In my own journey, I knew I'd need an MBA (at the time anyway) as well as a variety of experiences if I'd want to be known as a "master marketer," and I knew I would need specific kinds of experiences as I honed my positioning through the years to be a "builder and a fixer." By the way, I didn't know all of that upfront; it's been an evolution.

An ever evolving ten-year plan!

Because I knew that "dad" was part of my brand as well, I knew there were certain decisions I needed to make to have that achievement. Being a parent is a big decision and a big part of personal branding, so that too takes planning, just like any career.

This isn't manipulative and calculating; it's just that the big decisions in your life should be a part of the planning process for your brand.

Take a look at Kim Kardashian.

Say what you will, but the woman is a business, a brand, and an empire. Although it looks as if she lives a spontaneous life, I highly suspect that it has taken a lot of planning to get her where she is, both in her personal life and in her professional life.

The fact that her personal life is her professional life makes it all the more complicated. When you are a branded personality, it's even more important to plan out every move. I'll bet she operates just like a brand, or she wouldn't be seeing the kind of success she has.

Kim Kardashian is honestly as big as some of the big brands we see at the grocery store. She didn't have it all right from the start, but she did know what she was missing and went out and got it.

One of the things that the big brands do, as part of the annual planning process, is a *gap analysis*.

The brand managers make a list of their goals (one, three, five, and ten years) and then outline the assets they will need to achieve those goals. Some of those assets are already in hand, so they check them off the list. Others need to be achieved over a course of time.

Part of the gap analysis includes an overview of what needs to happen in order to gain that asset in that amount of time, in order to achieve your plan.

I knew I needed an MBA to achieve my brand goals, so my gap analysis included that education as well as a timeline of how I was going to get it (college GPA, application process, GMAT, raising tuition money, managing jobs, etc.).

Again, I wouldn't look out more than ten years because then it does get over-whelming and becomes almost inaction-able.

The gap analysis starts with the goals you've outlined, lists the assets you will need, checks off the ones you've already got, and then details how to get the others. Simple, right?

Perhaps another little chart, similar to the goal setting chart from the last chapter, will help. Start by putting your positioning statement right at the top, and then simply fill in the cells. If you don't know everything quite yet, that's okay. This is a work in progress.

My Personal Gap Analysis

Positioning Statement

Goal	Completed	Missing	Action Plan

Can you see how clear and concise this all becomes? When you put your mind to it, it honestly doesn't take that much effort.

Here's of what my gap analysis looks like. I love being a work in progress; it's what gets me up early every morning.

My Personal Gap Analysis
Marketing Master—Builder & Fixer

Goal	Completed	Missing	Action Plan
• Get experience launching new products	• Johnson & Johnson • Arm & Hammer	• Learn new categories in B2B and Technology	• Create a list of new business opportunities in B2B and Technology and research contact names to begin networking
• Start my own agency	• CP Partners		
• Write a book	• *The Experience Effect* • *The Experience Effect for Small Business* • *The Personal Experience Effect*	• Think of my next book concept	• Do a review of current business books to find gaps in the marketplace
• Become a global CEO	• President, North America for Cohn & Wolfe	• Move to next level to run a global organization	• Run global accounts • Conduct global new business pitches • Learn more about global markets

The key to all of this is to close the gaps, so that you can get all you need for your brand plan, which is how the gap analysis becomes more of an action plan and to-do list.

Simply use this gap analysis as a way to checklist the items you need to get done to complete your brand, and then move on to the next set of items.

It becomes a flowchart for building your *Personal Experience Effect*, with the ability to grow and change over time. Oh, that's the next chapter!

NOTES

9 Be Flexible

Hillary
Rodham
Clinton:
Results
Maker,
Despite the
Odds

All this planning and gap analysis is enough to make me dizzy. We can't be spending all of our time planning, or we'll never have time to enjoy the life that we're planning. We have to live in the moment and consider what is happening to us right now.

Life isn't just about planning, and neither is personal branding.

We need to have the ability to react to what's around us and to simply change our mind. We have to be able to change our course, often on a moment's notice.

The big brands do this all the time.

When a new competitor enters the market, it may force a new strategy and new approach to the market.

When forces in the economy affect demand, it may require a new product formulation or a new pricing strategy.

When consumer sentiment takes a pop culture turn, it may require a new messaging strategy.

Every good marketer knows that a big part of marketing is being flexible and responding to what's happening in the marketplace. The same is true of your personal brand.

First of all, you could change your mind.

It's your prerogative; it's your brand and your life. Heck, changing your mind might even be a part of your brand! As you go through your life, you may find that you're not happy with your path, and that's more than appropriate. In fact, it should be somewhat expected.

Your primary relationship may not have been what you planned.

The amazing job that you thought was going to set your direction for the next three years might not be living up to your plan.

Almost anything in your plan could have changed, and you need to be able to respond.

Life may not be turning out the way you expected, and you may have to change your brand and/or change your plans. That's okay; embrace it and be flexible.

You're a brand, and brands evolve. So then change it up. There's a reason your brand plan gets updated every year. You may not feel the same way that you did last year.

Anyone who has gone through a painful (or even not so painful) divorce knows that sometimes things just don't work out how you've planned. Any milestone event (like a divorce) requires a reworking of your plan. Treat it like an opportunity to replan your life. Doing that alone will help make you feel productive.

Or perhaps an opportunity comes along that you simply must take advantage of—it just might make sense to seize it, even if it wasn't in your plan.

I'm sure some of you may be thinking, *This doesn't apply to me.* Not true. I can guarantee that something in the world you're living in will change, which will force you to change your plans.

Be ready for it, and you'll grow from it.

Look at Hillary Rodham Clinton, one of the most successful women in politics with a rightful place in American politics and history.

She has certainly lived a life of extremes, under extreme scrutiny with both fans and foes around her. If you have followed her life, you see that it has had many twists and turns, and much of what she planned to do did not necessarily come to fruition at first. So she re-planned.

> Like when she tackled health care reform during her first term as first lady.

> Like when she became a senator from New York, which was not her home state.

> Like when she lost the presidential election to Barack Obama and then became his secretary of state.

Each of these events required a lot of planning and then replanning, and I don't think each of the outcomes was necessarily in her original plans. She evolved along the way, continually updating her one, three, five, and ten-year horizons. Or so it seems. I don't think we've seen the last of her brand.

Me?

I went to grad school at Columbia University for an MBA in marketing. Back in the day, Columbia had a good marketing program, but it was really known for its amazing finance program. Most people went to Columbia Business School for finance. I minored in finance because I knew it was such a good program.

As a marketing major, I was a bit of an anomaly, although there were many others just like me, fortunately.

In my first year of grad school, 1987, the stock market crashed. That was the big crash that everyone compared our more recent market swings to—it was so bad that it became the benchmark for bad.

The year 1987 was an interesting year to enter business school in New York City.

Many people called into question their choice of a career in finance or Wall Street, and marketing became a reliable career option for students who had never considered it before. Finance people who had never dreamed of a career in marketing were suddenly investigating it.

Like everything else, the economy swung back around, and I'm sure many people continued to pursue their finance aspirations. But I remember that many didn't. Many people took the economic effect seriously and changed their brands in response.

I can also remember back when I was going to start my own agency.

I was putting together the plans, figuring out how I was going to put it all together and launch it. In the middle of the process, a mutual colleague set me up with someone who was very familiar with launching new agencies, and I decided to go down a path with him.

It wasn't how I had originally planned, but it turned out to be a good opportunity, so I seized it. I changed my plans pretty much overnight.

In that case, I didn't really change my brand, but I did change the plan to get me there. I took advantage of an opportunity that was placed in front of me even though I hadn't anticipated it. It still accomplished my goals, however.

Truth be told, I had a lot of things going on in my life that required me to change my life dramatically. At the time, I needed to get out of the big company environment and into something more flexible. I had two small kids, and the big corporate job wasn't going to work anymore because I needed to be around for them. So I made a change to my original plan of a big corporate job. Not a change to my brand, but a change to my plan

Fortunately, it worked at the time.

So when an opportunity came along with a better way to create my agency, I grabbed it. My mind was open to how to get started, as long as I got it all going.

Meanwhile, fifteen years later, I'm back to the big corporate job. Irony? No, I'm still the same brand, just with a flexible plan. My kids are older, so I have the ability to do what I need to do for my career, and that is taking priority. And I'm adding other elements to my elevator pitch, like being an author and a professor, to enhance where I want my brand to go. I am rounding out my *Personal Experience Effect.*

The lesson learned here is to remain open, positive, flexible, and adaptive throughout the whole process. Having a plan in place doesn't mean that you put your head down and stop paying attention to what's happening around you. You may need to make a change.

Something may be happening right before your eyes that makes your plan inappropriate. You have to be ready, willing, and able to capture anything that comes along—on the fly.

Keep in mind that it may not require a change to your brand, or maybe it does. Either way, be open to the possibilities, and you'll maximize the opportunities in your life.

I've worked on many products where right before we launched a new campaign, our competitor did something that rendered our plans useless. Back to square one, but as marketing professionals, we were always ready for such a scenario and rolled with it.

You need to do the same, whether it's because you changed your mind or because something happened around you to require a shift in your plan.

It may also not be your plan that changes.

You may decide to make a fundamental change to your brand. You may want to be a different kind of person, a different brand, or you may want to highlight something that you never thought important before. You can evolve your brand over time.

After all, it's your choice, your life, and your brand.

I've seen many parents quit their highly successful jobs after having children. In many cases, they were the same people who swore that they'd never leave their jobs. They decided to make a fundamental change to their brand, and I know many who never went back.

Good for them.

I've also known many people who didn't want drugs, smoking, or alcohol to be a part of their brand anymore, so they changed who they were to change their brand and their life.

It's also good to evolve your brand over time.

Grow your brand as you grow as a person. Change with the times; grow as our culture grows, and enhance your brand with opportunities that come your way. Seize the opportunities to grow in a multitude of directions.

There is one big piece of advice, however, that you must keep in mind along the way.

Hang on to the connections and relationships you've developed through the years, at each part of your elevator pitch.

These people not only make up a part of your brand but also carry you from milestone to milestone. I still have many of the friendships I created in college—during my first job at Johnson & Johnson and when I ran Saatchi & Saatchi Wellness—as examples.

These are the relationships that make Jim Joseph and that inspire me to continually move to the next phase of my brand. Those of you who know me know that I've been very aggressive with my career. Without all of my colleagues by my side, I never would have been able to do each aggressive step.

My colleagues are a part of my builder and fixer brand.

I encourage you to do the same.

Social media makes keeping connected to people so much easier than ever before. We'll talk about it a lot in the next chapter, but staying active in the various social media outlets will help keep you connected to those you've let into your life.

Keep them in your life, and don't be afraid to let new people in either.

I know a lot of people who are completely satisfied with who they have in their network of colleagues and friends and are almost afraid to let in anyone new. I think that's foolish. Adding new people into your life helps grow your brand.

New people almost always force you to be flexible, and we all need a nudge every so often.

Make sure you are adding new people and new experiences to your brand on an ongoing basis. These are the things that will help your brand evolve and will help you decide if you truly are on the right course for your brand.

They will also help you see if your brand needs adjusting, something you may not be able to see for yourself.

That's what friends are for!

NOTES

10 Own the Digital World

Michael J. Fox: Accomplished Activist, Awarded Actor

We talked in the last chapter about how important it is to stay connected with people and that social media has become an amazing tool to help us all do that.

In this chapter, we're going to talk about how the digital world can really enhance your brand. Actually, how in some cases, the digital world is your brand.

The digital space gives us an opportunity to stay connected with one another, all the time. Among Facebook, Twitter, and LinkedIn, I communicate with friends and colleagues virtually every day from the entire spectrum of my life—from grade school right through to my current job. It's amazing and brings me such joy.

When I see any of these folks IRL (in real life), it's as if we never got out of touch. It's wonderful.

This is all so very good for my brand too.

The digital world has given me a voice for my craft.

It's really and truly made me the builder and fixer that I profess to be. Every morning I write a blog post, and then I use social media to publish it. As a result, folks whom I would never really come in contact with are able to read and learn about marketing. Non-marketers follow me because they say they learn a lot from my marketing stories.

Without the digital world, my brand would be very different. I wouldn't have the same reach or impact.

I recently went to a reunion party with some of my colleagues from Johnson & Johnson, many of whom I had not seen in close to twenty years. Because many of us are on Facebook, it was instant re-connection. We could ask real, relevant questions about one another's lives. And they were all in tune with what was going on with my brand.

In fact, in many ways they are my brand. They not only helped build my marketing experience but are also the ones commenting and promoting my books and blog posts. They are my references when I look to make a career move.

They are my brand because we are all connected on the digital landscape.

I love citing Michael J. Fox as one of my favorite personal brands, partly because he's my generation, and he too grew up without all the digital tools we now have. But, like me, he's learned to embrace them and love them.

He has a personal mission, very much tied to his own elevator pitch, which has become his brand. He mixes traditional resources along with digital ones to get his message across, and he's incredibly consistent in his messaging.

You know who Michael J. Fox is, whether you meet him in person or online. The digital world has helped him to not only continue to build his brand, but also to continue to build his brand followers.

Using the digital world isn't just about social media and building a base of fans and followers, though. There are many other ways that the digital world helps us as well.

Whenever I need something at work that I can't figure out, I simply do a search on LinkedIn and I'm pretty much guaranteed to find someone who knows something that will help me out. I get numerous similar requests from people in my network on a weekly basis. It's a great vehicle to help one another out.

In helping out my son's brand—he needed a calculus tutor—I instantly found a tutor online who had taken the same class with the same teacher. The tutor is amazing, and I couldn't help but notice that he's a brand in development himself.

The digital world is particularly useful at key milestones in our lives because we can research ways to connect with people. My high school friends were coming out in droves when my daughter graduated from high school, which was so much fun. It was a wonderful reminder of what was at the time the beginning of all of our brands.

Obviously, on social media, you can post your own point of view, your pictures, things that you care about, and arguments you'd like to make.

Facebook, as an example, is a wonderful way to showcase your brand. Every comment, picture, check-in, link, and like is a statement about your brand. The sum is a reflection of who you are. Post purposefully.

In fact, your behavior on social media becomes your brand. While the digital world is a platform for your brand, use it with care because there can be a fine line between productive and destructive behavior.

When used wisely, social media is like a stage you can perform on.

When used incorrectly, it can damage your brand in a New York minute.

Be careful about what you post, be cautious about the photos you publish, and be purposeful about who you let in. Every interaction is your brand, so be consistent with your brand positioning and with the followers you have gathered.

Consistency is key.

Even the people you follow can be a reflection of your brand, so be purposeful about that as well. Remember that it's all a permanent record; once someone else shares it, then it's out in the world and out of your control.

Choose your topics wisely based on your brand definition.

Because my social media outlets are so public, I really try to stay away from politics and religion. They are not a part of my brand anyway. I remember one time I did share a post from Tina Fey, not even realizing that I was making a political statement as a result. I didn't think I even said much other than how much I love her, and it started a firestorm on my Facebook page.

I even got a comment about my personal life, posted in response to my love of Tina Fey. It had gone too far for my taste.

It was a lesson learned in public behavior even though it wasn't intentional on my part. Every single post you make is a reflection of your brand, and people are evaluating it as such. Think before you click.

I learned at that Tina Fey moment that everything I do in social media must be consistent with my brand, or I leave it alone. Even during the election, I was super careful about what I posted. When I share others' points of view, those too are a reflection of my brand, so I am careful about that as well.

I've learned these lessons the hard way, many times over. I once shared an article about gun control only because it featured an argument that I had not heard before. A virtual war took place on my Facebook page as a result, which clearly reflected upon my brand.

Part of it I didn't mind because I consider myself a connector (or builder) of people and networks. If they want to use my social media platforms to discuss, then that's also a part of my brand. But from a branding perspective, I'd rather have them do it on topics that are closer to my brand positioning.

I'd prefer to keep it positive.

If having a political point of view on social issues is a part of your brand, then social media is a perfect place. I have many friends where politics and social issues are a big part of who they are, and I love following them and listening to their points of view. It's their brand, and I love them for it.

The point here is to be purposeful and consistent with your brand at every step.

NOTES

11 Find Your Voice, Choose Your Look

Jack Welch:
Businessman
Extraordinaire

We talked a lot about social media in the last chapter and how it can shape and become your brand—depending on how you behave. This is a relatively new phenomenon in marketing, whether we are talking big brand marketing or personal branding.

Those before us didn't have to deal with all the issues that come with social media—the good and the bad. They didn't have to worry about the instantaneous nature of what we say and post, nor did they have to deal with the issues of personal privacy.

They didn't have to worry about everything they do being shared and commented upon.

But we do. Which is why we have to use social media, and all aspects of our personal brand, with great caution.

It all starts by finding your voice.

A fundamental part of our journey here is to find your voice in social media and in all aspects of your brand. Your overall tonality—how you do and say things and even how you look—are all a reflection of your brand, and on your brand.

Proceed with deliberate caution.

Part of defining your brand, as we've been discussing, is finding your voice.

Is your brand patient and kind, or is it rushed and emphatic?

Is your brand all-knowing or all seeking?

Is your brand comedic or sarcastic, or somewhat serious?

This may sound too theoretical, but trust me, it's not.

The language you use and your tone of voice is very influential in how people perceive you, and how they therefore formulate opinions about your brand, which then becomes your brand.

Take a look at *The Real Housewives* franchise of shows on Bravo. Each of those women (or characters actually) is a brand. They are all on the show for a reason—to promote their brand; whether to sell books or liquor or anything else in between, the women on that show are each a brand. I've even heard them say it!

Our perceptions of their brands are definitely shaped not only by their behaviors and actions, but also by their voice—meaning, how they talk, how they say things, and how they carry themselves.

Take a look at Jack Welch, businessman extraordinaire. This man's voice is his own, and it's incredibly consistent, so much so that his tone and manner have become his brand.

Think about your own interactions with people around you.

When a person is constantly cursing, even if he/she is the nicest person in the world, his/her brand reflects negativity and meanness. It just does.

When someone speaks loudly and shouts over people all of the time, that too says something about his/her brand.

When someone is super quiet and hardly ever says anything, then we are going to decide what his/her brand is all about too.

We can't help ourselves.

This is particularly true on social media because all we have is our voice on these channels. There are no hand gestures or facial expressions to supplement our language and how we talk, so we have to be very careful and deliberate.

What we post becomes who we are.

I make a concerted effort to constantly be positive in my posts. In fact, on the rare occasion that I get a little snarky, it takes people off guard. On the other hand, I have friends who are constantly snarky, and we expect that from them.

We love them for it.

I even have a few friends who have multiple characters in social media—one is nice, one is naughty, etc., but they use different social channels to express themselves. Yet within each profile, they consistently use the same voice to represent that part of their brand.

They are able to express themselves differently in each voice while still keeping each of their brand profiles.

You have to consciously choose your voice because in many ways, it becomes your brand. So you should make sure that your voice is true to how you've positioned your brand and how you want others to perceive you.

Make your voice an active part of your brand, knowing that people are evaluating it. Be consistent!

There's nothing more confusing than someone bouncing all over the place in tonality and in how he/she conducts himself/herself. Be true to your brand, all of the time, each and every time.

Something that goes hand in hand with your brand voice is how you look.

Personal grooming, clothing, accessories, and even your home and car are a part of your brand. We could write entire books on personalizing your home to match your brand and also how to pick a car to match your brand.

It's important to consciously think about how your look is perceived and how it adds to (or detracts from) your brand.

Me?

I'm into color and patterns, and I like to make a statement in how I dress. I try not to do too much at once; one gimmick at a time as they say. But I am very determined in choosing my look, and I shop accordingly.

Every day (okay, most days) I think about what's going on and pick a look for the day.

> Sometimes it's jeans, a sports coat, and a patterned shirt (my complete uniform).

> Sometimes it's a suit (when I need to show the serious side of my brand).

> Sometimes it's a sweater and khakis.

> Sometimes it's a tie with a bright shirt and jeans.

> Sometimes it's a hoodie with a shirt and tie.

Every combination is uniquely Jim Joseph though, partially because it's a conscious choice to include how I look into my brand voice.

I've had many people tell me that while they are shopping, they often see clothes and think of me. That's the sign of a firmly defined brand, and I love it.

I'm not suggesting that you suddenly become a clotheshorse. It depends on your brand. But I am suggesting that you be purposeful about it. Wearing worn T-shirts and jeans every day is only okay if it somehow matches your brand.

It's funny because in some ways, people are really into this topic. Whenever I write a blog post about personal style, it is always the most read and most commented post of the month.

I've covered:

- how to wear jeans

- what a hat adds to your look

- how to tie a scarf

- whether it's okay to wear swimwear to the gym

It's fun commenting on personal style and how it builds your brand. I'm not a fashion stylist, just a marketing master, so I look at it from that perspective.

What do you wear?

Are your clothes a conscious choice?

Do they match your brand and your brand choice?

If you've never thought about any of this before, then perhaps you should add "changing my look" to your brand gap analysis.

Remember that there's no one more successful looking than someone who looks as if he/she puts care into his/her look. No matter what the look is, it's your brand.

When your brand looks successful, then it's likely to be so.

NOTES

Chapter

12 Go to Market

Cher:
The Ultimate
Survivor

Now that we've done all our homework for our brand, it's time to take it out into the marketplace. It's time to live it. You've defined your brand and have a positioning statement that best captures it. You've written out your goals, and you have a one, three, five, and ten-year plan.

You are ready to go, so jump right in.

If you are in search of a new job, a new home, a new mate, whatever the case may be, it's time to live your brand. Remember to make consistent choices, based on what your brand is all about and based on what you've decided you want out of life.

What's important to remember is that you are on display—via social media, in a job interview, on a first date, whatever the situation.

You are out on display, as a person and as a brand.

This shouldn't intimidate you; it should excite you. There's nothing to be nervous about. You've done your homework: you know who you are, you know what you want, and you know what you need to do to get there.

Bravo! Now live it.

Take a look at Cher.

She is the ultimate survivor in the entertainment world. I believe she is one of only a handful of entertainers who have had music releases in the '60s, '70s, '80s, '90s, '00s, and '10s. She knows who she is, and being a survivor in that industry is a big part of her brand.

She references it all the time.

She is in no way afraid to live it. She puts herself out there, she changes along the way, and she's not shy about it. She is living her brand on her terms, and she makes no apologies.

Her followers love her for it.

When you are first exposed to her, she takes a bit of getting used to. But that too is a part of her brand. In Cher's case, her first impression is quite bold, and also something she creates quite purposefully.

I'd like you to think about your first impression and how you take your brand to market.

There's an old saying about first impressions: "You never get the chance to do them over." That is so true, and never truer than today. The greater truth now is that first impressions are either completely over in a nanosecond or happen before you ever meet anyone.

We've become very quick to judge society, or at least our judgments are much quicker and more public.

With social media, first impressions are already made before you ever enter the room. You either have to make your social media first impression a positive one or you'll spend the bulk of your time overcoming it.

Something as simple as your profile picture creates a first impression, so even that should be purposeful. I had a boss who always told me, "No pictures with alcohol in them," for that very reason. Unless you are a master sommelier and understanding wine is a part of your brand.

I can speak from experience when it comes to interviewing.

I definitely look up people on social media to check out their brand—to see if they are complementary to my own brand and my company's brand. I do this so I have some sort of an idea of what they are like before I actually meet them. It's my way of determining a first impression, before the live first impression in the job interview.

I then often go back on social media after I've met the person, particularly on LinkedIn and Twitter. I want to see their industry presence, their level of social activity, and their point of view. I also want to see if they have been consistent in their interview questions with how they actually live their life.

I am not the only person who does this, trust me.

Your life is being evaluated with every milestone you make.

It's important to realize that people are picking and sorting you based on your brand. I know it sounds cold, but it's true. You probably do it too. As long as you know your brand, know what you want, and know what you need to do, you have nothing to worry about.

Nothing at all.

And go out and relish being on display. You've built your brand well, so it's time to put it in motion. Don't be afraid to test-drive a few ideas. You need to be flexible with your brand so you can see what works and what doesn't work with your plan.

I know that I do this on social media a lot.

I've learned through the months and years what kinds of things my followers like, and in what channel they like them. Pictures are more for Facebook and Pinterest. Articles about the industry belong on Twitter. Because I consider my followers to be a part of my brand, I often follow their lead in terms of what they like. I rarely post personal notes on Twitter, as an example, because they generally go unnoticed.

It's quite a different experience on Facebook.

Through trial and error, I've learned the topics that resonate the most, so I focus on them to build my brand.

The folks on Facebook like more personal things from me, like pictures and commentary. The folks on Twitter, like more industry topics from me. I only figured that out by living my brand and by experimenting.

It's the fun part of being a brand. Go out and live yours!

NOTES

Chapter
13 Surround Yourself

Arnold Schwarzenegger: First Muscleman

The whole point of this book, beyond the theory of personal branding, is to get what you want out of life, both personally and professionally. The goal is to find out what makes you happy, and then go out and get it.

Set your goals, and then set your sights on making them all happen. In order to do that, you need to have a focus and a mission, and that mission should be to bring your brand to life.

You have to know what you want—that's part of the goal setting we've talked about—and be flexible over time.

Remember that this is a process—a long and hard process that happens over the course of a lifetime. Continue to prioritize and stay focused, and you will be successful. Your definition of success may change over time, but you will be successful.

It's also important to surround yourself with people who add to your brand and to your brand experience. The people you associate with help to define your brand.

I would not be Jim Joseph without my kids, my partner, my friends, and my colleagues. My brand wouldn't exist without them.

Your friends, in many ways, become your brand. Even your followers on social media are a reflection of your brand. I wouldn't have the kind of brand that I have without my social media connections; they've become a big part of who I am, and they have become a big part of my brand experience.

I have quite a few people on my social networks who are very vocal, and while I don't necessarily agree with their points of view, I love that they are there. Having a network of people who add commentary to life is a part of my brand. But it may not be a part of yours, so you have to make those decisions about the kind of people you want in your life.

You have to decide what you want.

People who are very vocal about social issues on your social media sites may not add to your brand. In fact, if potential employers saw them there, they may make a flash decision (first impression) about you.

You have to decide what you want.

Even more importantly, though, you want people around you who support your brand. You want people around you who will help you get what you want out of life and will help you make your one, three, five, and ten-year goals.

You have to decide what you want.

It's not that you are being manipulative; it's just that you need to be strategic in the choices you make about the people around you.

Look at Arnold Schwarzenegger.

Throughout his entire career, he has surrounded himself with people who advance his brand. Talk about a brand that has been flexible and that has evolved! From his early days as one of the first weight lifters to his career in politics, his team has propelled him. I am sure, beyond just love, it was a very conscious choice to marry Maria Shriver, given her political/media brand and his political brand aspirations.

Arnold Schwarzenegger knows what he wants.

You should do the same.

Make an honest assessment of those around you, and make some decisions about how they can support your brand. Friends who provide a fun atmosphere are also supporting your brand. I have many people in my life who do that for me, and vice versa, and I am indebted to them for it. They lighten me up.

They, too, are a part of my brand.

I would recommend that you write it out. Make a "brand support list" of all the people in your life and how they support and grow your brand, or make some decisions about how they could be supporting your brand.

Those who don't support your brand, perhaps should not be in your life. If you have gaps, then perhaps there's a way to find people who can be more supportive in different ways.

Maybe you can try to find a mentor at work, or you can join a trade association if you don't have enough people in your life who are supporting your career and your brand aspirations in that way.

Here's a format you could use:

My Personal Team List

Goal	People I Know	People I Need	Action Plan

Chapter 13: Surround Yourself

In filling this out, you will have to ask yourself some tough questions:

Will my boss support me in my goals?

Have I communicated my plans to my significant other, and has he/she bought into it?

Do my friends take me off my game because they always want to party?

Ask yourself some tough questions, and be prepared for the answers. You may not like them at first, but if you stick to your brand plan, then you know you'll be doing the right thing.

It's easy to delay this kind of stuff because it can be somewhat confrontational. You may not like the answers you give to yourself, and you have to face that. You may not be surrounded by the right people, and you might not know what to do about it.

Or you may not have enough people around you, supporting your brand.

Take it one day at a time. Start by knowing what you want, and then surround yourself with others who will help get you there.

You can't create and evolve your brand in a day; that's why your marketing plan includes a ten-year horizon. Map out the decisions you need to make, and put a time frame on them.

Some of your decisions may take years to implement, and that's okay. You've got a plan, and you know what you want out of life, no matter how long it takes.

The key is to get started. Today. Surrounding yourself with the right people is a key part of building your plan.

NOTES

14 | Make Your Mark

One of the biggest trends in big brand marketing is called *purpose*. Some call it "marketing with a purpose," some call it "brand purpose," and some call it "cause marketing."

No matter what you call it, it's becoming all the rage to have meaning behind your brand. A brand should not just be about selling stuff. A brand needs to give back.

This isn't anything new, but the notion of purposeful marketing caught on big with the brand TOMS shoes. The essence behind the TOMS brand is "buy one, give one"; for every pair of shoes you buy, another pair goes to a child in need.

"Buy one, give one" is TOMS sole purpose (pun intended).

"Buy one, give one" isn't just a promotion for the brand; it's a natural part of the brand itself. The brand was created to give shoes to children, and then a business plan was modeled to deliver against it. It was fancied by the owner and CEO, Blake Mycoskie, because this particular cause is very near and dear to his heart.

He created the TOMS brand with a mission in mind, and it wasn't just to sell shoes. Selling shoes is the means to the end for this brand.

Bill Gates also has a purpose. Sure, he is one of the biggest success stories in business history, but his personal brand is so much more than that. His Bill & Melinda Gates Foundation gives back millions, and some say he is the biggest philanthropist in the country.

This isn't just about charity. It's about giving back. It's about putting a purpose into your personal brand so you stand for something more than just yourself.

For some, this could be giving back to your community or helping the next generation or supporting a cause that's close to your family.

This is about making your mark, not just having personal success. It's all about doing good for those around you.

This should not be a bolt on. Having a brand purpose needs to be a natural part of your brand definition and a definitive part of your brand. You need to bake it into your positioning statement and weave it into your plans.

Part of my brand purpose is to give to the next generation of marketers. That is why I teach and write so much; it's my way of giving back, and it's built right into my brand definition. Or, better said, I have evolved into my brand definition through the years.

I don't teach and write to make money because that's not the motivation or the result, quite honestly. I do it to help the next generation of marketers who are trying to learn and perhaps don't have access to the kinds of mentors I was so lucky to have.

By sharing my experiences, I hope they can become better marketers. I also spend a lot of time doing informational interviews and speaking engagements at industry events and college campuses. I meet with new folks coming into marketing all the time.

Giving to the next generation gives my brand a purpose. It helps me live out being a builder and a fixer.

You should do the same.

Add a purpose to your brand so you rise above yourself and give your brand meaning. Create a way to give back.

Give it a way to make your mark, and make it a personal part of your personal brand.

Best of luck to you. See you online.

NOTES

A Story of Inspiration

**Two Tweets,
One Brand**

I wanted to conclude my book with a story about someone who is on the journey of creating a personal brand—someone who felt inspired to create a life for herself, knew what she wanted to be, and set out to get it. It turns out I found two people, not just one, and they started their journey at an interesting time in their (at that point) separate lives. "Marketing is a spectator sport," so I hope you learn something from the personal brands of Sandi and Rick and their Midlife Road Trip.

The MidLife Road Trip began like many other brands—with notes on a paper napkin. Only ours was a modern-day napkin known as Twitter. What began as a simple conversation bouncing back and forth like a virtual ping-pong match has become a full-time career.

In the beginning:

Rick Griffin had a life-threatening illness that forced him to evaluate what he would do moving forward. Once recovered, he vowed that he was going to start doing everything he had ever wanted to do and start checking things off his bucket list.

Sandi McKenna was in search of the next chapter, the next phase in her life. Having spent several years in the sandwich generation, wedged in between aging parents and growing children, she was looking for a creative outlet.

Twitter was in its early years. It was before brands and celebrities found it fashionable or before the hashtag was in vogue. It was a great place for conversation and chatting with like-minded people. A simple conversation began with a small group of virtual friends about producing a video. Show ideas and the potential for developing it into something more substantial soon followed. It really was that basic. It was brainstorming in 140 characters.

Sandi was living in Tampa, Florida, at the time and Rick was living in Atlanta, Georgia with his family. We were fleshing out the concept before we ever actually met. Even our tagline "Therapy for a MidLife Crisis" was created virtually.

It was months before we actually met in person. Rick, his wife, and his daughters were heading to Tampa on spring break and met Sandi for coffee. It was that meeting that set the course for the future. We decided we would bring our vision to life and shoot a pilot episode. Loosely scripted, the initial episode was the groundwork for what we could do and where we could go with this, our very own personal brand. Our business plan was in its most basic form. We had an idea and a vision, so we ran with it. We didn't realize we were creating a brand, but we did have our very own "Field of Dreams." We thought, Let's build it and they will come.

Up until this point, nobody knew what we could do with it. At the time, I'm not sure we knew what we could do either, but our brand was born.

What we did know:

We knew we wanted to tell stories.

We knew we wanted to create great videos that would include travel and adventure. It wasn't until later in the process that we added food. We had no idea at the time what a big part culinary travel would eventually play in our brand story.

We knew we wanted to bring together the virtual and real world.

We wanted to check things off our bucket lists and inspire others to do the same.

We wanted to incorporate a sense of humor and fun. Laughter is a big part of our brand.

We wanted to collaborate with other brands.

How we did it:

We created a product to show people what our vision was. Our very first video really defined who we were and set the tone for what viewers could expect from our brand.

Like many people, skydiving had long been on Rick's bucket list, so it was the perfect place to start. Rick leapt out of the plane, joking before, during, and after. Sandi was waiting on the ground, cracking wise jokes and eating a cookie. Here we introduced our personal brands that made up MidLife Road Trip. We established Rick as the daredevil and

Sandi as the sarcastic, sensible one (or at least in her mind). It resonated with others because we were ourselves.

We realized quickly that our flaws made us real and relatable. We decided to leave the outtakes in our videos. Not only was it a calculated move, but equally a necessity because we needed content, and we had so many outtakes! Viewers found our self-deprecating humor endearing because they saw who we really were, warts and all, not pretending to be anything other than what we were—two middle-aged people with a passion for food, travel, and adventure.

As Jim would say, we have stayed consistent. While our brand has grown and evolved, we have remained true to our original vision: creating a food, travel, and adventure series devoted to making the most of every moment. We never deviated from our core values nor compromised our integrity.

Our brand is a true reflection of who we are. We are our brand. The MidLife Road Trip is about us, about our personal journey navigating our way through midlife. With over eighty-one million baby boomers in the United States, we are not alone on this journey. What we do is give them a peek behind the curtain, showing them how they, too, can make the most of their midlife years.

We are your average Joe/Jo. Our brand shows how ordinary people can have extraordinary experiences.

When people watch Rick learn to surf for the first time, getting thrown about by crashing waves, they feel his pain. When Sandi meets her fear of flying head-on by taking a flying lesson in a small Cessna over Los Angeles, their palms sweat too. It is therapy for a midlife crisis.

How we measure our success:

We are four years into our ten-year plan. We are, in many instances, charting new territory. We have taken what began as a single tweet and created a lifestyle. We travel and we document it.

We focus on positive experiences. That's not to say bad or unpleasant things don't happen during our travels, but nobody wants to hear us rant about a missed connection due to delays, lost luggage, or even a lumpy bed. Our brand is about inspiring others. Ranting and raving—unless it's about bad coffee or wine (just kidding)—won't come from us!

We know we have hit our target when someone says, "You made us laugh" or "You put a smile on my face." There comes a time in life when you don't sweat the small stuff anymore. This is that time for us.

We have had the pleasure of interacting with some major brands that, in many ways, share our same values, like Southwest Airlines, Bing, Four Seasons, and Expedia. It has been a lesson in patience, waiting until the time and collaboration are the right fit. The way we naturally and organically use product placement has become our brand signature as well. By integrating like-minded brands into our videos, we have seamlessly been able to keep our personal and professional brands on track without compromising our integrity.

Ours is a tale of two tweets that transformed into a brand story of hope. Our brand is about stepping out of your comfort zone.

It's not only about dreaming, but dreaming big.

It's about inspiring others.

Embracing who you are.

Celebrating our differences.

Encouraging others.

Not taking yourself too seriously.

Having and expressing gratitude.

Finding joy in simple pleasures.

Riding out the tough times by knowing that there's something better on the horizon.

Our brand is about getting older, getting going, and giving it all you've got. Our brand is on a journey that has only just begun.

Sandi McKenna and Rick Griffin
Cohosts, MidLife Road Trip

About Jim Joseph

Jim Joseph:
A Builder and
a Fixer

Entrepreneur of the Year.

Agency of the Year.

Most Creative Agency.

Thought Leadership Certificate of Excellence.

Social Media Icon.

These are not accolades that Jim Joseph takes lightly or too seriously either. They inspire him everyday to continue to excel and to learn.

Jim Joseph is the kind of guy who actually watches the television commercials rather than skipping through them. He scans the magazine ads before ever reading the columns, hard copy and online. Don't be surprised to find him in his office, legs propped up, flipping through Twitter on his iPad.

As the President of Cohn & Wolfe North America, Jim brings over twenty-five years of consumer marketing leadership, bold management prowess, and a fine head of hair to the agency. If running this gig wasn't big enough, he's also a three-time author, blogger, professor at New York University, and regular contributor to *Entrepreneur* and *Huffington Post*. To top it off, he's on the Board of Directors for the number one branding school in the country, The Brand Center at VCU, as well as The Council of PR Firms and DTC Perspectives.

When you want to get something done, give it to someone who's busy!

Jim's brand pedigree is a portfolio in the who's who of marketing, including Tylenol, Johnson & Johnson, IKEA, Cadillac, Ambien, Nokia, Walmart, and Kellogg's. His entrepreneurial streak motivated him to start his own agency after years of client side marketing at Johnson & Johnson and Arm & Hammer.

He later sold that agency to The Publicis Groupe, where he managed agencies covering brand strategy, consumer promotion, shopper marketing, digital, CRM, and advertising.

With the strength of a power-lifting honey badger and the intelligence of, well, an NYU professor, Jim's boldest move transformed what was a struggling pharmaceutical advertising agency into an integrated marketing powerhouse, Saatchi & Saatchi Wellness. Jim engineered a makeover that included new capabilities in CRM, promotion, and digital, as well as a new mix of clients beyond pharma into diverse areas of wellness.

Fulfilling a lifelong dream, Jim published his first marketing book in 2010 called *The Experience Effect*, which showed how building a powerful brand experience creates shareable consumer loyalty. As Jim says, "Without a great brand experience, you're just another product." The book garnered much critical acclaim, winning a Silver Medal for Best Marketing Book from Axiom.

Sequels take a look at applying that big brand theory to small business with *The Experience Effect for Small Business* and personal branding with *The Personal Experience Effect*. His daily blog and continuing contributions to *Entrepreneur* remind us that "marketing is a spectator sport," as he touches on big brand experiences as well as advice for anyone in marketing, even if you are just marketing yourself.

Following Jim is like following the best that the marketing industry has to offer because that's who he watches and reports on every day.

Other THiNKaha® Books

Purchase these books at THiNKaha **http://happyabout.com** or at other online and physical bookstores.

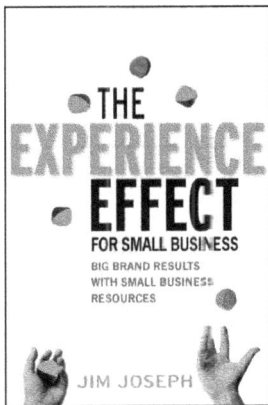	***The Experience Effect For Small Business*** Jim believes that there's simply no reason why a small business cannot perform like a big brand, even within our turbulent times. His perspective makes this book is a timely and compelling read. Hardcover: $29.95 eBook: $14.95
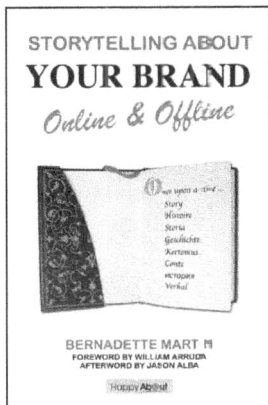	***Storytelling About Your Brand Online & Offline*** Using this book, professionals and executives of all types, entrepreneurs, consultants, musicians, academics, and students, will undergo a "personal branding process." Paperback: $22.95 eBook: $16.95

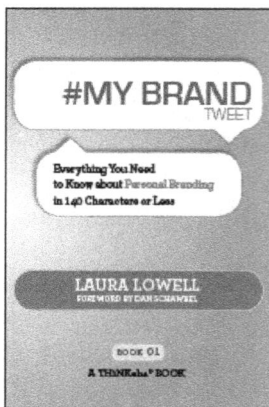

#MYBRAND tweet Book01

If you are new to the idea of personal branding, have toyed with the idea of creating a personal brand, or simply wish to take your career to the next level, this book is your first step toward differentiating yourself in a very crowded environment.

Paperback: $19.95
eBook: $14.95

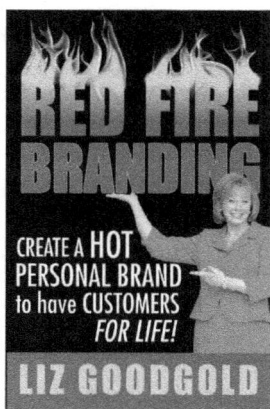

Red Fire Branding

Liz Goodgold directs her works toward the business-to-business market to help small business owners, entrepreneurs, sales professionals, or anyone who is looking to create an indelible image.

Hardcover: $39.95
Paperback: $19.95
eBook: $14.95

9781600052415